Measurement of Engineering Properties of Soils

Measurement of Engineering Properties of Soils

E. Saibaba Reddy
B.Tech., M.E., Ph.D.
Professor and Head
Civil Engineering Department
Jawaharlal Nehru Technciogical University
College of Engineering, Hyderabad

K. Rama Sastri
B.E., M.E., Ph.D.
Professor, Civil Engineering
and Rector
Jawaharlal Nehru Technological University
Hyderabad

PUBLISHING FOR ONE WORLD

NEW AGE INTERNATIONAL (P) LIMITED, PUBLISHERS
New Delhi • Bangalore • Chennai • Cochin • Guwahati • Hyderabad
Jalandhar • Kolkata • Lucknow • Mumbai • Ranchi
Visit us at www.newagepublishers.com

Published by New Age International (P) Ltd., Publishers
First Edition: 2002
Reprint: 2010

Branches:

- No. 37/10, 8th Cross (Near Hanuman Temple), Azad Nagar, Chamrajpet, **Bangalore**- 560 018.Tel.: (080) 26756823, Telefax: 26756820 E-mail: bangalore@newagepublishers.com
- 26, Damodaran Street, T. Nagar, **Chennai**- 600 017. Tel.: (044) 24353401, Telefax: 24351463, E-mail: chennai@newagepublishers.com
- CC-39/1016, Carrier Station Road, Ernakulam South, **Cochin**- 682 016. Tel.: (0484) 2377004, Telefax: 4051303, E-mail: cochin@newagepublishers.com
- Hemsen Complex, Mohd. Shah Road, Paltan Bazar, Near Starline Hotel, **Guwahati**- 781 008, Tel.: (0361) 2513881, Telefax: 2543669 E-mail: guwahati@newagepublishers.com
- No. 105, 1st Floor, Madhiray Kaveri Tower, 3-2-19, Azam Jahi Road, Nimboliadda, **Hyderabad**- 500 027. Tel.: (040) 24652456, Telefax: 24652457 E-mail:hyderabad@newagepublishers.com
- RDB Chambers (Formerly Lotus Cinema)106A, 1st Floor, S.N. Banerjee Road, **Kolkata**-700 014, Tel.: (033) 22273773, Telefax: 22275247 E-mail:kolkata@newagepublishers.com
- 16-A, Jopling Road, **Lucknow**- 226 001. Tel.: (0522) 2209578, 4045297, Telefax: 2204098, E-mail: lucknow@newagepublishers.com
- 142C, Victor House, Ground Floor, N.M. Joshi Marg, Lower Parel, **Mumbai**- 400 013, Tel.: (022) 24927869, Telefax: 24915415 E-mail: mumbai@newagepublishers.com
- 22, Golden House, Daryaganj, **New Delhi**- 110 002. Tel.: (011) 23262370, 23262368, Telefax: 43551305, E-mail: sales@newagepublishers.com

ISBN : 978-81-224-1413-4

Rs. 135.00

C-10-07-4793

Printed in India at A.H. Print Pack, Delhi.

PUBLISHING FOR ONE WORLD
NEW AGE INTERNATIONAL (P) LIMITED, PUBLISHERS
4835/24, Ansari Road, Daryaganj, New Delhi-110002
Visit us at **www.newagepublishers.com**

PREFACE

Geotechnical Engineering deals with the projects associated with soil and rock formations. Accurate measurement of engineering properties of soil plays a very important role in the design and execution of these projects. The soil is either used as construction material (as in earthen dams), supporting material (as in foundations) or as surrounding material as in tunnels etc. Further, the soil will be subjected to different types of loads—static or dynamic or cyclic. The engineering properties to be measured depend on the type of project and nature of soil (cohesive or non-cohesive).

The objective of this book is to classify the soil tests, method of selection tests under various conditions and test procedures for 30 laboratory and field tests to measure engineering properties of soils including the dynamic properties.

A set of questions is presented at the end of each chapter for self examination of the test procedure and the theory behind each experiment.

It is hoped that this book will be useful to B.Tech. (Civil Engg.), M.Tech (Geotech. Engg.) and research students. It is also hoped that this book will be of help to practising engineers in deciding about the specific test for a case.

Authors sincerely invite suggestions from students, faculty and practising engineers for improving the book's quality and presentation.

The authors wish to express their thanks to the New Age International Publishers for bringing out the book in such a nice form. Authors wish to express their special thanks to the family members of the senior author—Sudha Reddy, Satish Reddy and Rakesh Reddy who supported and helped in the different stages of writing of this book.

E. Saibaba Reddy
K. Rama Sastri

CONTENTS

1

INTRODUCTION

1.1 INTRODUCTION

Soil is an essential construction material for civil engineers. Hence, the accurate measurement of soil properties is very important in the design and execution of a civil engineering project. The use of soil varies depending on the type of projects. Soil is used as (*i*) construction material (Example: roadways, railways, earthen embankments, earthen dams), (*ii*) Supporting material (Example: Foundations) and (*iii*) Surrounding material (Example: Underground pipelines, tunnels). Different properties of soil need to be measured depending on the type of project. Soil is a natural material and hence its properties varies considerably from place to place. For example, the behaviour of clay soils depends on its plasticity and stiffness. The behaviour of sandy soils depends on its particle size distribution, angle of internal friction and relative density. Therefore, engineer needs to measure the specific property of soil, depending on the type of project and the nature of soil. The type of structure depends on the purpose for which it is constructed. Classification tests identify the type of soil. Hence, in any soil testing programme the preliminary tests involve classification tests. Based on the type of soil and nature of the project a detailed test programme is planned. The following sections present the need and the means of identifying the testing programme.

1.2 NEED FOR SOIL TESTING

Soil testing is an essential part of a civil engineering project, the failure of a project due to improper/inadequate soil testing is very expensive and some times irreparable. Hence, understanding the properties of soil and its consideration in the design are important.

The three important aspects in soil testing programm are:

1. Identification of appropriate soil test.
2. Accurate measurement of soil properties.
3. Analysis of test data and interpretation of properties for the design of structure.

The soil testing aspects listed at points 1 and 3 above mostly depend on the experience and engineering judgement of the problem and the point 2 depends on the care taken during the testing.

Unlike steel or concrete, for which a set of properties are available depending on their grade, soils show different properties at different locations and it is not possible to state the properties of the soil without measuring them either in the field or in the laboratory. The important aspect of soil testing is that, it is not simple to prepare a common list of tests to be performed for all projects. This is because, the soil properties to be measured depends on the type of soil and the nature of project.

1.3 IDENTIFICATION OF TESTS

Identification of appropriate tests is the most important aspect in the soil testing programme. The required tests for a given project depend on

1. The nature of the project.
2. The nature of the soil.

1.3.1 Nature of project

The tests to be performed on soil depend on the nature of project for which it is being utilized. The important civil engineering projects where soil properties considered are:

1. Earthen embankment to store water
2. Road construction
3. Foundation
4. Filling behind a retaining wall

The following sections explains how a testing programme is planned based on the nature of project.

Earthen embankment: Construction of an earthen embankment involves identification of site for the construction of the structure and the location of source of soil for construction. The suitable soil is borrowed from a nearby area (known as borrow pit area). The identification of soil suitability for the construction of earthen embankment depends upon soil type and permeability. This is ascertain by conducting classification and permeability tests. After identifying the soil to be used for the construction, one need to know its physical, compaction and shear properties. Compaction properties include optimum moisture content (OMC– the moisture content that is required to be added to the soil while compaction to attain maximum dry density) and the corresponding maximum dry density that can be achieved for the soil. The OMC and the maximum dry density of soil are estimated by conducting compaction tests (standard proctor compaction test or heavy compaction test, see chapters 18 & 21). Shear strength properties viz. Cohesion, C and angle of internal friction, ϕ of soil helps in the design of embankment section from stability criteria. Shear strength properties are estimated by conducting shear tests such as Direct shear test or Triaxial test or unconfined compression test or vane shear test on the soil samples compacted at OMC conditions. Permeability properties of soil are also measured for the compacted soil to study the hydraulic properties such as drainage characteristics, phreatic line, flow net and estimation of flow through embankment and exit hydraulic gradient of flow. The shear and permeability properties used in the design (which are based on laboratory compacted samples) need to be verified by conducting the tests on core soil samples collected from the embankment during construction. Hence, it can be stated that in the construction of an earthen embankment, the tests used are (1) Classification tests i.e. grain size distribution tests, Atterberg's Limit Tests (2) Proctor compaction test (3) Density tests and (4) Shear tests. Hence for the construction of an earthen embankment the above mentioned tests are required.

Road Construction: For the construction of a road embankment, the tests to be performed on the soil include the tests recommended for the earthen embankment. Further, there is a need to perform California Bearing Ratio (CBR) test (see chapter 20 & 28) for the design of flexible pavements and plate load test (to obtain modulus of sub-grade reaction K-see chapter 27) for the design of rigid pavements.

Foundations: For the design of foundation, the geotechnical engineer needs to suggest depth and type of foundation and an allowable bearing capacity of the soil. This is done, by obtaining the shear and settlement properties of soil. This is done, by obtaining the shear and settlement properties of soil. The soil properties at different depths are obtained by advancing bore holes or excavating trial pits and performing field and/or laboratory tests. The tests generally performed in the field include Standard Penetration Tests (SPTs), dynamic cone penetration tests and Plate Load Tests (PLTs). The tests performed in the laboratory for the foundation design include the test to estimate shear parameters cohesion C and angle of internal friction ϕ. These parameters are obtained by performing either Vane shear test or unconfined compression test or direct shear test or triaxial test. Further, to estimate allowable bearing pressure from settlement criterion there is a need to estimate the consolidation properties of soil such as coefficient of consolidation C_v and compression index C_c. In special situations such as foundations on Black Cotton (BC) soil the swelling and shrinking properties are also need to be measured.

Retaining wall: To design a retaining wall, the soil pressure acting on back of the wall needs to be estimated. To estimate the soil pressure unit weight of the soil, cohesion and angle of internal friction are to be measured. Similar properties are required to measure the stresses acting on the underground structure to arrive at appropriate design.

Machine foundations and earthquake analysis: For the design of machine foundations and earthquake analysis of foundations, there is a need to estimate dynamic properties of soil such as coefficient of uniform compression C_u, coefficient of uniform shear C_τ, damping coefficient ξ, Young's modulus, E and shear modulus, G of soil. For the measurement of these properties, dynamic testing of soils such as block vibration tests; wave propagation tests and/or cyclic plate load test are to be performed.

1.3.2 Nature of soil

Soil testing not only depends on the type of the project as explained above but also on the type of the soil. For example, laboratory tests are preferred for clay soils and field tests are preferred for coarse-grained soils. Similarly, in laboratory tests, Atterberg's limit tests and Hydrometer analysis tests are used to classify clay soils and Sieve analysis test is used to classify the coarse grained soil. Shear parameters of clay soils are measured by performing either unconfined compression tests or Vane shear test or Direct shear test or Triaxial shear test. But the shear parameters of a sandy soil are obtained either from direct shear test or triaxial shear test. Similarly the strain rate used for clay soils is small compared to coarse-grained soil. The difference in rate of testing is due to drainage conditions. In clay soils the permeability (hydraulic conductivity) is very low therefore large pore pressures are developed during shear and hence it needs more time for dissipation. Further, in foundation analysis, settlement studies such as consolidation tests are necessary for clay soils. This is because, clay soils has more porosity and low permeability. More porosity means more amount of settlement and less permeability means more time required for the complete settlements to occur. Hence, to estimate the settlement behaviour of foundation, consolidation tests will be performed on clay soils. Similarly, swelling properties are observed in clay soils and not in sandy soils.

The compactness of cohesive soils is measured in terms of OMC conditions (by performing compaction test) and the same is represented in terms of relative density (by conducting minimum and maximum density tests) in case of sandy soils.

This book is divided into three sections. The Section-I deals with classification of tests on soil and basic definitions and relationships used in soil mechanics. Section-II presents the details of laboratory tests used for soil testing. Field tests including dynamic testing of soils are presented in Section III.

2

CLASSIFICATION OF TESTS

2.1 INTRODUCTION

There are a number of tests available to measure the engineering properties of soils in laboratory and field. The tests to be performed depend on the type of soil and the nature of project. Tests can broadly be classified as laboratory tests and field tests.

2.2 LABORATORY TESTS

Laboratory tests are performed on soil samples collected from field. The samples are either collected in an undisturbed state, in the form of core samples, or in a disturbed state, in the form of loose soils collected in bags. The disturbed soil samples are used to perform classification tests. The undisturbed soil samples are used to perform tests to obtain majority of its engineering properties of soil such as strength, consolidation, permeability, density, moisture content etc.. The laboratory tests, classified for the purpose for which the soil is being used are as follows:

1. Classification tests
2. Test to obtain physical properties of soil
3. Shear tests
4. Compressibility tests
5. Other specific tests

2.2.1 Classification Test

The tests to be performed on a soil depends on the type of soil (i.e. cohesive or non-cohesive soils) and nature of project. Performing classification tests helps to assess the type of soil.

The classification test involves.

1. Grain size distribution
   (a) Sieve analysis
   (b) Hydrometer
2. Tests for Atterberg's limits
   (a) Liquid limit tests
   (b) Plastic limit tests
   (c) Shrinkage limit tests

The sieve analysis test results are used to classify the coarse grained soils such as sand and gravel. The Hydrometer analysis and the Atterberg's limit test results are used to classify fine grained soils such as silt and clay.

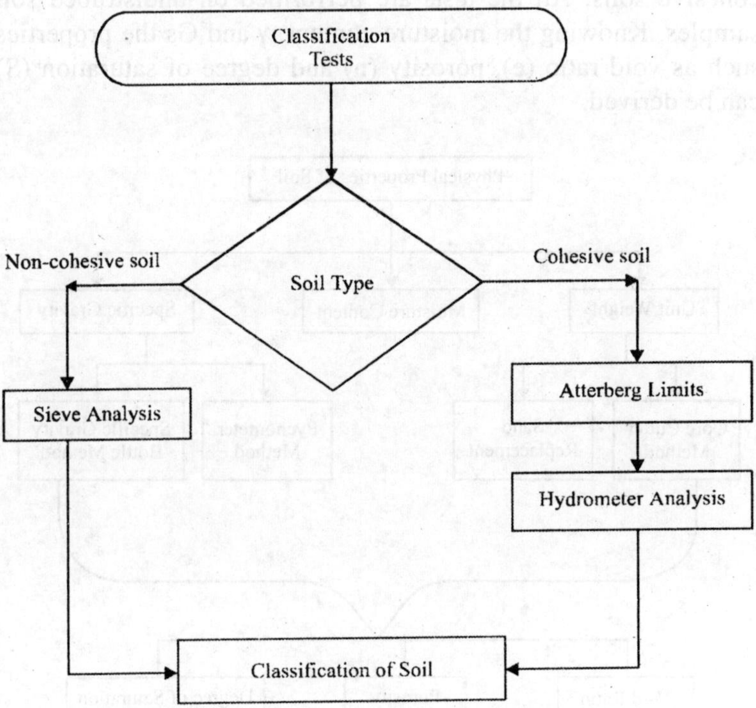

***Figure 2.1* : Flowchart for Classification Tests**

2.2.2 Tests to obtain physical properties of soil

The physical properties of soils include moisture content (m), unit weight (γ), specific gravity (Gs), void ratio (e), porosity (n), degree of saturation (S), etc. The tests to obtain these properties are:

1. Moisture content test
2. Specific gravity test
3. Field density tests by core cutter method
4. Field density test by sand replacement method

Moisture content and specific gravity tests are performed on all soil samples. The test (3) and (4) are used to obtain density of soil. The core cutter (3) is used for soils having cohesion and the sand replacement method is suitable for both cohesive and non-cohesive soils. All the tests are performed on undistrubed soil samples. Knowing the moisture content, γ and Gs the properties such as void ratio (e), porosity (n) and degree of saturation (S) can be derived.

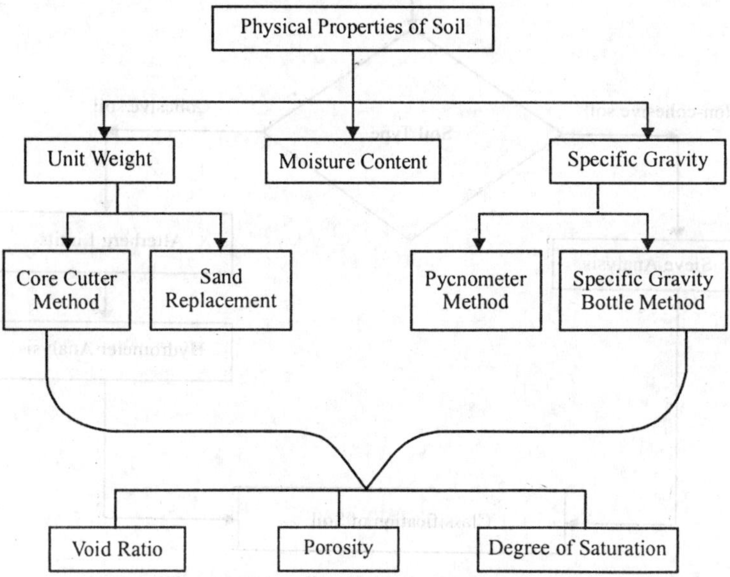

Figure 2.2 : **Flowchart for Strength properties**

2.2.3 Shear tests

Stability of soil structures (i.e. foundations, embankments, road structures, canal slopes etc.) depends on the shear resistance of soils. Shear resistance of soil is dependent of the two shear parameters of soil i.e. cohesion(C) and angle of internal friction (ϕ). Cohesion is due to plastic nature of soil, clay soils are more plastic. Therefore the clay soils are also known as C-soils. Internal friction of a soil is due to frictional resistance developed between adjacent particles due to roughness of particles and moving of particles one over the other. Internal friction is observed mainly in coarse-grained soils such as sand and gravel. The sandy soils and gravelly soils are also called ϕ – soils. In practice most of the soils have both C and ϕ.

A number of tests are available to obtain shear parameters of soil. All the tests are performed on undisturbed soil samples. If undistrubed samples are not available remoulded samples prepared at field density are used for testing. The various tests available to obtain shear parameters of soil are:

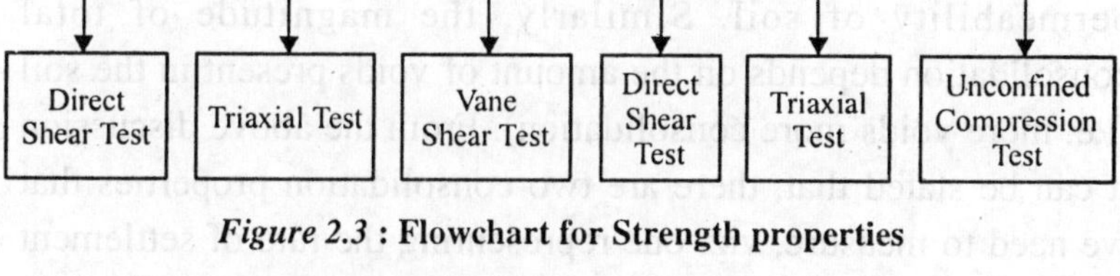

Figure 2.3 **: Flowchart for Strength properties**

1. Triaxial shear test (used for clay or sand)
2. Direct shear test (clay or sand)
3. Vane shear test (clay only)
4. Unconfined compression test (clay only)

The selection of test depends on the required accuracy and available time. For example, using the triaxial shear test apparatus three types of tests (i.e. unconsolidated undrained test (UU), consolidated undrained (CU) test and consolidated drained test (CD)) can be performed by controlling the drainage conditions of the sample. An UU test is completed in shortest time about 1 hour and a CD test takes a long time (a few days) to complete. Direct shear test, Vane shear and unconfined compression tests are quick but they provide less accurate results. Hence, for less important structure and for quick assessment of properties the tests listed under (2), (3), and (4) are employed. More details on these experiments are presented in later chapters.

2.2.4 Compressibility tests

Compressibility or consolidation is the property of soil due to which the soil undergoes reduction in volume under a constant weight. During the process of consolidation (mainly studied in saturated soils) the voids in the soil reduces due to expulsion of water from the voids under an applied constant compressive load. Therefore the rate of reduction in voids (rate of consolidation) depends on the easiness with which the water moves through the soil. The ability of soil to allow a liquid to pass through it is termed as permeability (hydraulic conductivity). Therefore rate of settlement/consolidation is directly proportional to the permeability of soil. Similarly, the magnitude of total consolidation depends on the amount of voids present in the soil (i.e. more voids more consolidation). From the above discussion it can be stated that, there are two consolidation properties that we need to measure, viz. one representing the rate of settlement and the other representing the total settlements. The consolidation tests commonly used are:

1. to determine compression index (C_c)
2. to determine coefficient of consolidation (C_v)

Clay soils have low permeability and large void ratio. That means in clays rate of consolidation is low and total consolidation is large. Hence, the consolidation properties are studied in clay soils rather than in sands which has more permeability.

The apparatus used for the above experiments is the same (consolidation test) only the testing procedure changes. The details of these tests are presented in Chapters 12 & 13.

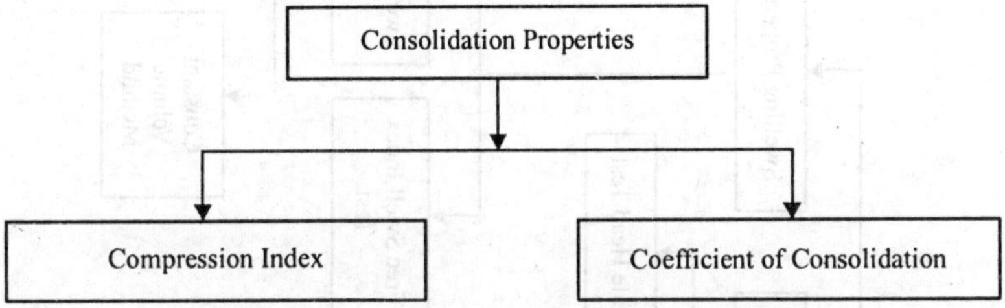

Figure 2.4 **: Flowchart for Consolidation Properties**

2.2.5 Other special tests

Besides the conventional tests explainèd above, a few tests are performed specially to suit the requirements of a particular field appliction. The following tests are considered under this classification.

1. California bearing ratio test (for flexible pavement design)
2. Permeability tests (for seepage analysis)
3. Compaction test (embankment design)
4. Relative density test (to estimate compactness of non-cohesive soils)
5. Swelling tests (to estimate the swell potential of the soil and uplift pressure on foundation)
6. Linear shrinkage test

Besides these, there are also a number of tests such as chemical analysis of soils, tests to determine organic contents, tests to determine total dissolvable solids etc.

The classification of tests and guidelines to select an appropriate test based on soil type is explained in the form of flow chart in Figs. 2.1 to 2.5.

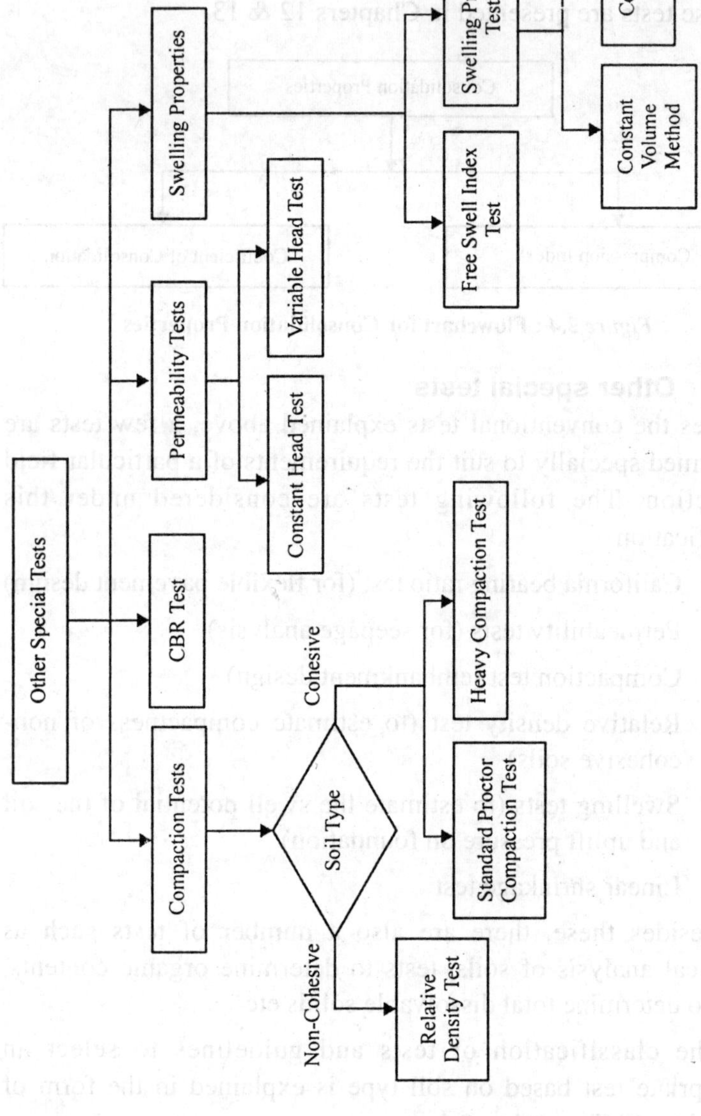

***Figure 2.5* : Flowchart for Special Tests**

2.3 FIELD TESTS

The laboratory tests are convenient to perform as they are performed in fully equipped laboratory and in controlled conditions. However, as the laboratory tests are performed on the soil samples collected from the field, the reliability of these test results depends upon the quality of soil samples collected. A reasonably good undisturbed soil sample can be collected from clay layer. If the soil at the site is non-cohesive, it is difficult to obtain a good undisturbed soil sample. Hence, the tests performed at the site are always considered reliable for sandy soils. Hence, a balanced soil test programme involves a large number of laboratory tests supported by a reasonable number of field tests.

Field tests are mainly designed to obtain strength parameters used for foundation and pavement design. Further, a few field tests are available to study the properties of soil under dynamic loads used for the design of machine foundations and earthquake studies. Hence the field tests are broadly classified as:

1. Field tests for foundations
2. Field tests for pavement design
3. Field tests to determine dynamic properties of soil

2.3.1 Field tests for foundation design

The following tests are useful in measuring the strength of soil in the field to estimate the bearing capacity of soils for foundation design.

1. Standard penetration test. (SPT)
2. Dynamic cone penetration tests (DCPT)
3. Static cone penetration test
4. Field vane shear test
5. Plate load test (PLT)

The first four tests are useful in measuring the strength of soil along the depth. These tests enable to estimate the bearing capacity of foundations. Further test (1) and (2) are more suitable for sandy soils and the test (3) and (4) are recommended for clay soils. The plate load test (5) is also used for the estimation of bearing capacity of soil. However, this test is expensive. Therefore, it is not advised to perform at different depth. The plate load test is generally performed at foundation level. This test is considered as confirmatory test.

2.3.2 Field tests for pavement design

The commonly used field tests to obtain soil parameters required for designs of pavements are

1. Field CBR
2. Plate load test

Field CBR test gives the CBR valves of soil in the field conditions. The CBR valves are useful in the design of flexible pavement. Plate load test is performed in the field to obtain the coefficient of sub-grade modulus. The sub-grade modulus of soil is used in the design of rigid pavement and apron.

2.3.3 Field tests to determine dynamic properties of soil

For the design of machine foundations and to study the behaviour of structures under earthquake loading we need to measure the dynamic properties of soil. The commonly measured dynamic properties of the soil are coefficient of elastic uniform compression (C_u), coefficient of elastic uniform shear (C_τ) and damping ratio (ξ). These properties are obtained by performing dynamic tests on soil. The dynamic tests on of soil also enables to measure elastic properties such as Young's modulus (E) and shear modulus (G) of soil. The following tests are performed to measure various dynamic properties of soil.

1. Cyclic plate load test
2. Block vibration test (vertical vibrations)
3. Block vibration test (horizontal vibrations)
4. Steady state vibration test

The details of these tests and the computation procedure used to compute various dynamic properties of soils are explained in Chapters 29-32.

3

SYMBOLS AND DEFINITIONS

3.1 INTRODUCTION

This book deals with a number of tests for engineering properties of soil and their related literature. It is therefore appropriate to give definition of different terms used in this book. Though the definition of each term is presented at its first appearance, this chapter helps as ready reference of any term used in this book.

GLOSSARY OF TERMS AND SYMBOLS RELATING TO SOIL

F = Force

L = Length

T = Time

D = Dimensionless

Where synonymous terms are cross-referenced, the definition is included with the earlier terms alphabetically. Where this is not the case, the later term is the more significant.

Absorbed water : Water held mechanically (by surface tension) in a soil mass.

Activity : Ratio of the plasticity index to the clay fraction.

Adhesion : Shearing resistance between soil and another material under zero externally applied pressure:

	Symbol	***Unit***
Unit adhesion	c_a	FL^{-2}
Total adhesion	C_a	F or FL^{-1}

Adsorbed Water : Water in a soil mass, held by physico-chemical forces, having physical properties are substantially different from absorbed or free water or chemically combined water at the same temperature and pressure.

Air Void Ratio e_a, (D) : The ratio of the volume of the air space to the volume of solids, in a soil mass.

Allowable Bearing pressure (Gross), q_a (Gross) (FL^{-2}) : The maximum allowable gross loading intensity on the ground on any given case, taking into account the maximum safe bearing capacity (gross), the amount and the kind of settlement expected, and the ability of the given structure to take up this settlement. It is, therefore, a combined function of both the site conditions and characteristics of the particular structure it is proposed to erect thereon.

Allowable Bearing Pressure (Nett), q_a (Nett) (FL^{-2}) : The allowable bearing pressure (gross) minus the surcharge.

Allowable Pile Bearing Load (Allowable Load on Pile), Q_a (F) : The load which may be safely applied to a pile after taking into account its ultimate bearing resistance, pile spacing, overall bearing capacity of the ground below the piles and allowable settlement.

Angle of Internal Friction (Angle of Shearing Resistance), ϕ (Degrees) : Angle between the abscissa and the tangent to the curve representing the relationship between the shearing resistance at failure to the normal stress acting within a soil.

Angle of Repose, α (Degrees) : Angle between the horizontal and the maximum slope that a soil assumes through natural processes. For granular soils, the effect of height of slope is negligible; for cohesive soils, the effect of height of slope is so great that the angle of repose is meaning less.

Angle of Wall Friction, δ : Angle between the abscissa and the tangent of the curve representing the relationship of shearing resistance to normal stress acting between soil and surface of another material.

Area Ratio of a Sampling Spoon, Sampler or Sampling Tube, A_r (D) : The area ratio is an indication of the volume of soil displaced by the sampler in proportion to the volume of the sample, calculated as follows:

$$Ar(\%) = (D_e^2 - D_i^2)/D_i^2 \times 100$$

where

D_e = maximum external diameter of the sampling spoon, and

D_i = minimum internal diameter of the sampling spoon at the cutting edge.

Bearing Capacity Factor (D) : Non dimensional factors for the computation of bearing capacity.

Bearing Capacity, Maximum Safe, q_o (FL^{-2}) : The maximum intensity of loading that the soil will safely carry with a factor of safety against shear failure irrespective of any settlement that may result.

Black Cotton soil : Black cotton soils are inorganic clays of medium to high compressibility and forms a major soil group in India. They are predominantly Montmorillonitic in structure and black or blackish grey in colour. They are characterized by high shrinkage and swelling properties.

Boulder : A more or less rounded block or fragment of rock and of average dimension 300 mm or greater. Usually boulders are rounded by being carried or rolled along by water or ice; sometimes also by weathering in place in which case they are known as boulders of weathering, disintegration or exploration.

Bulking : The increase in volume of a material due to handling. Rock bulk upon excavation; damp sand bulk if loosely deposited, as by dumping, because the apparent cohesion prevents movement of the soil particles to form a reduced volume.

California Bearing Ratio, CBR (D) : The ratio of the force per unit area required to penetrate a soil mass with a circular piston of 50 mm diameter at the rate of 1.25 mm/min to that required for the corresponding penetration of a standard material. The ratio is usually determined for penetrations of 2.5 mm and 5 mm. Where the ratio at 5 mm is consistently higher than that at 2.5 mm, the ratio at 5 mm is used.

Capillary Water : Water subject to the influence of capillary action.

Clay : An aggregate of microscopic and submicroscopic particles derived from the chemical decomposition and disintegration of rock constituents. It is plastic within a moderate to wide range of water content.

Clay Size : That portion of the soil finer than 0.002 mm.

Cobble : A rock fragment, usually rounded or semi-rounded, with an average dimension between 80 and 300 mm.

Coefficient of Compressibility (Coefficient of Compression) (a_v) (L_2F^{-1})

- The secant slope, for a given pressure increment of the effective pressure
- void ratio curve.

Coefficient of Consolidation, C_v (L^2T^{-1}) : A coefficient utilized in the theory of consolidation, containing the physical constants of a soil affecting its rate of volume change:

$C_v = K(1 + e)/(a_v\gamma_w)$

Where

K = coefficient of permeability, LT^{-1};

e = void ratio, D;

a_v = coefficient of compressibility, L^2F^{-1}; and

γ_w = unit weight of water, FL^{-3}.

Coefficient of Curvature (C_c) : It is given by

$C_c = (D_{30})^2/((D_{10}) X (D_{60}))$

Where D_{10}, D_{30}, and D_{60} are the diameters of particles corresponding to 10, 30 and 60 percent finer respectively.

Coefficient of Earth Pressure, K (D) : The ratio between the lateral effective pressure and vertical effective pressure, at any point in the soil mass.

Coefficient of Earth Pressure, Active, K_a (D) : The smallest value of coefficient of earth pressure resulting when the soil expands laterally till failure.

Coefficient of Earth Pressure, at Rest, K_o (D) : Value of coefficient of earth pressure when the soil is permitted neither to expand nor compress laterally.

Coefficient of Earth Pressure, Passive, K_p (D) : The maximum value of coefficient of earth pressure resulting when the soil is compressed laterally thereby inducing failure in the soil.

Coefficient of Permeability (Permeability), K (LT^{-1}) : The rate of flow of water under laminar flow conditions through a unit cross-sectional area of porous medium under a unit hydraulic gradient and standard temperature conditions.

Coefficient of Subgrade Reaction (Modulus of Subgrade reaction), K (FL^{-3}) : Ratio of load per unit area (applied through a centrally loaded rigid body) of horizontal surface of a mass of soil to corresponding settlement of the surface. It is determined as the slope of the secant draw between the point corresponding to zero settlement and the point of 1.25mm settlement, of a load – settlement curve obtained from a plate load test on a soil using a 75 cm or greater loading plate.

Coefficient of Uniformity, C_u (D) : The ratio D_{60}/D_{10}, where D_{60} is the particle diameter corresponding to 60 percent finer on the grain – size curve and D_{10} is the particle diameter corresponding to 10 percent finer on the grain – size curve.

Coefficient of Volume Compressibility (Modulus of Volume Change), m_v, ($L^{-2}F^{-1}$) : The compression of a soil layer per unit of original thickness due to a given unit increase in pressure. It is numerically equal to the coefficient of compressibility divided by one plus the original void ratio, or

$$m_v = a_v/(1 + e)$$

Cohesion, c (FL^{-2}) : The portion of the shear strength of a soil indicated by the term c, in Coulomb's equation, $\tau = c + \sigma \tan\phi$.

Cohesion, Apparent : Cohesion in granular soil due to capillary forces.

Cohesionless Soils : A soil that, when unconfined, has little or no strength when air-dried and that has little or no cohesion when submerged.

Cohesive Soils : A soil that, when unconfined, has considerable strength when air-dried and that has significant cohesion when submerged.

Compaction : The densification of a soil by means of mechanical manipulation.

Compaction Curve (Moisture – Density Curve) – The curve showing the relationship between the dry unit weight (density) and the water content of a soil for a given compaction effort.

Compaction Test (Moisture – Density Test) : A laboratory compaction test procedure whereby a soil at a known water content is placed in a specified manner into a mould of given dimensions, subjected to a compaction effort of controlled magnitude and the resulting unit weight determined. The procedure is repeated for various water contents sufficient to establish a relation between water content and dry unit weight.

Compressibility : Property of a soil pertaining to its susceptibility to decrease in volume, when subjected to load.

Compression Index, C_c (D) : The slope of the linear portion of the pressure – void ratio curve on a semi-log plot, with the pressure on the log scale.

Consistency : The degree of resistance offered by a fine-grained soil to deformation.

Consistency Index (relative Consistency), I_c (D) : Ratio of the liquid limit minus the natural water content to the plasticity index of a soil:

I_c = (LL-Nm)/(PI)

where

LL = liquid limit

Nm = natural moisture content

PI = plasticity index.

Consolidated:Drain Test (Slow Shear Test) : A soil test in which a soil specimen is first allowed to consolidate fully under an applied stress and shear stresses are then applied in such a manner that there is full dissipation of excess pore water pressure developed during shear.

Consolidated-Undrained test (Consolidated Quick Test) : In this case, the soil is consolidated under applied normal loads but no drainage of water from the soil is permitted to take place during shear.

Consolidation : The gradual reduction in volume of a soil mass partly or fully staturated resulting from an increase in and continued application of compressive stress and is due to the expulsion of water from the pores.

Initial Consolidation (Initial Compression) : A comparatively sudden reduction in volume of a soil mass under an applied load due principally to expulsion and compression of gas in the soil voids preceding primary consolidation.

Primary Consolidation (Primary Compression) : The reduction in a volume of a soil mass caused by the application of a sustained load to the mass. This is due principally to squeezing out of water from the void spaces of the mass and accompanied by a transfer of the load from the soil water to the soil solids.

Secondary Consolidation (Secondary Compression) : The reduction in volume of soil mass caused by the application of a sustained load to the mass. This is due principally to the adjustment to the internal structure of the soil mass after most of the load has been transferred from the soil water to the soil solids.

Consolidation Ratio, U_z (D) : The ratio of the amount of consolidation at a given point within the subsoil and at a given time to the total amount of consolidation obtainable at that point under a given stress increment.

Contact Pressure, p (FL^{-2}) : The soil reaction per unit area at the surface of contact between the foundation and the underlying soil-mass, produced by the self weight of the foundation and all the forces acting on it.

Controlled Strain Test : A test in which the load is so applied that a controlled rate of strain results (a test in which a specified rate of deformation is applied and the reaction to this deformation is measured).

Creep : The time dependent deformation behaviour of soil under constant compressive stress.

Critical Circle (Critical Surface) : The sliding surface assumed in a theoretical analysis of the stability of a soil mass for which the factor of safety is a minimum.

Critical Density : The unit weight of a saturated granular material below which it will lose strength and above which it will gain strength when subjected to rapid deformation.

Critical Height, H_c (L) : The maximum height at which a vertical or sloped bank of soil will stand unsupported under a given set of conditions.

Critical Slope : The maximum angle with the horizontal at which a sloped bank of soil of given height will stand unsupported.

Critical Void Ratio, E_c (D) : Void ratio prior to the process of shear in which nett volume change at failure is zero.

Deflocculating Agent (Deflocculant) (Dispersing Agent) : An agent that prevents fine soil particles in suspension from coalescing to form flocs.

Degree of Compaction, D_c (D) : The ratio of dry density of compacted material in the field to the laboratory standard maximum dry density of the material multiplied by 100.

Degree of Consolidation (Percent Consolidaton), U(D) : The ratio; expressed as a percentage of the amount of consolidation at a given time, within a soil mass to the total amount of consolidation obtainable under a given stress condition.

Degree of Saturation (Percent Saturation), S_r (D) : The ratio, expressed as a percentage, of the volume of water in a given soil mass to the total volume of voids.

Density Index (Relative Density) (Degree of Density), I_D (D) : The ratio of the difference between the void ratio of a cohesionless soil in the loosest state and any given void ratio, to the difference between its void ratios in the loosest and in the densest states:

$I_D = (e_{max} - e) / e_{max} - e_{min}) \text{ X } 100$

where

e_{max} = void ratio in loosest state,

e = void ratio in the field, and

e_{min} = void ratio in its densest state obtained in the laboratory.

Deviator Stress σ_d (FL^{-2}) : The difference between the major and minor principal stresses in a triaxial test.

Dilatancy : The expansion of cohesionless soils when subjected to shear deformation.

Direct Shear Test : A shear test in which soil under an applied normal load is stressed to failure by moving one section of the soil container (shear box) relative to the other section.

Discharge Velocity, v (LT^{-1}) : Rate of discharge of water through a porous medium per unit of total area perpendicular to the direction of flow.

Dry Density (Dry Unit Weight), γ_d (FL^{-3}) : The weight of oven dry soil per unit volume of soil mass.

Earth Pressure : The pressure or force exerted by soil on any boundary:

	Symbol	*Unit*
Pressure	p	FL^{-2}
Force	P	FL^{-1}

Active Earth Pressure, P_a, p_a **:** The minimum value of earth pressure. This condition will exists when a soil mass is permitted to yield sufficiently to cause its internal shearing resistance along with a potential failure surface to be completely mobilized.

Earth Pressure at Rest, P_o, p_o **:** The value of the earth pressure when the soil mass is in its natural state without having been permitted to yield or without having been compressed.

Passive Earth Pressure, P_p, p_p **:** The maximum value of earth pressure. This condition exists when a soil mass is compressed sufficiently to cause its internal shearing resistance along a potential failure surface to be completely mobilized.

Effective Diameter (Effective Size), D_{10} (L) : Particle diameter corresponding to 10 percent finer on the grain size curve.

Effective Force, (F) : The force transmitted through a soil mass by inter-granular pressure.

Exchange Capacity (Base Exchange Capacity) : The capacity to exchange ions as measured by the quantity of exchangeable ions in a soil.

Fines : Portion of a soil finer than 75-micron.

Floc : Loose, open structured mass formed in a suspension by the aggregation of minute particles.

Flow Curve : The locus of points obtained from a standard liquid limit test using the mechanical device plotted on a graph representing water content as ordinate on an arithmetic scale and the number of drops as abscissa on a logarithmic scale.

Flow Failure : Failure in which a soil mass moves over relatively long distances in a fluid-like manner.

Flow Index, I_f (D) : The slope of the flow curve obtained from a liquid limit test using the mechanical device (given by the difference in water contents at 10 blows and at 100 blows).

Flow Line : The path that a particle of water follows in its course of seepage under laminar flow conditions.

Flow Net : A graphical representation of flow lines and equipotential lines used in the study of seepage phenomena.

Flow Value, $N\phi$ (D) : A quantity, equal to $\tan^2 [45° + \phi/2]$ where ϕ is the angle of internal friction of soil.

Footing : A spread construction in brick work, masonry or concerete under the base of a wall or column for the purpose of distribution of load over a large area.

Foundation : That part of the structure which is in direct contact with and transmits loads to the ground.

Free Water (Gravitational Water) (Ground water) (Phreatic Water) : Water that is free to move through a soil mass under the influence of gravity.

Free Water Elevation (Water Table) (Ground Water

Surface) (Free Water Surface) (Ground Water Elevation) : Elevation at which the pressure in the ground water is zero with respect to the atmospheric pressure.

Frost Action : Freezing and thawing of moisture in materials and the resultant effects on these materials and on the structures of which they are a part or with which they are in contact.

Gradation (Grain-Size Distribution) (Soil Texture) : Proportion of material of each grain size present in a given soil.

Grain-Size Analysis (Mechanical analysis) : The process of determining gradation.

Gravel : Angular, rounded or semi-rounded particles of rock or soil of particle size between 4.75mm and 80mm.

Heave : Upward movement of soil caused by expansion or displacement resulting from phenomena, such as moisture absorption, removal of overburden, driving of piles, frost action and hydrostatic pressure.

Hydraulic Gradient, I, s(D) : The difference or drop of hydraulic head per unit distance of flow,

dh/dl

Critical Hydraulic Gradient, i_e (D) : Hydraulic gradient at which the inter-granular pressure in a mass of cohesionless soil is reduced to zero by the upward flow of water.

Hydraulic Pressure, u_o (FL^{-2}) : The pressure in a liquid under static conditions; the product of the unit weight of the liquid and the difference in elevation between the given point and the free water elevation.

Excess Hydrostatic Pressure u (FL^{-2}) : The pressure that exerts in pore water in excess of the hydrostatic pressure.

Linear Expansion, L_E (D) : The increase in one dimension of soil mass, expressed as a percentage of that dimension at the shrinkage limit, when the water content is increased from the shrinkage limit to a given water content.

Linear Shrinkage, L_s (D) : Decrease in one dimension of a soil mass, expressed as a percentage of the original dimension, when the water content is reduced from a given value to the shrinkage limit.

Liquidity Index (Water-Plasticity Ratio) (Relative Water Content), I_L (D) : The ratio expressed as a percentage of the natural water content of soil minus its plastic limit to its plasticity index.

Liquid Limit, w_L : The water content, expressed as a percentage of the weight of the oven dry soil, at the boundary between liquid and plastic states of consistency of soil.

Mohr Circle : A graphical representation of the stresses acting on the various planes at a given point.

Mohr Envelope (Rupture Envelope) (Failure Envelope) (Rupture Line) : The envelope of a series of Mohr circles representing stress conditions at failure for a given material. According to Mohr rupture hypothesis, a rupture envelope is the locus of points the co-ordinates of which represents the combinations of normal and shearing stresses that will cause a given material to fail.

Moisture Content (Water Content), w (D) : The ratio expressed as percentage of the weight of water in a given soil mass to the weight of solid particles under a specified testing condition.

Normally Consolidated Soil deposit : A soil deposit that has never been subjected to an effective pressure greater than the existing effective overburden pressure.

Optimum Water Content (Optimum Moisture Content), OMC (D) : The water content at which a soil can be compacted to the maximum dry unit weight by a given compaction effort.

Over-Consolidated Soil Deposit : A soil deposit that has been subjected to an effective pressure, which is greater than the present effective over-burden pressure.

Permeability : The property of soil which permits prcolation.

p^H (D) : The p^H value of hydrogen-ion concentration is a measure of the acidity or alkalinity (basicity) of a soil. It is expressed as $p^H = \log 1/(H^+)$
where H^+ = the hydrogen-ion concentration in moles/litre.

Phreatic Line : The upper free water surface of the zone of seepage.

Phreatic Surface : Free water surface of the zone of seepage.

Pile : Relatively slender structural element which is driven, or otherwise introduced, into the soil, usually for the purpose of providing vertical or lateral support.

Piping : The movement of soil particles by percolating water leading to internal erosion and the development of channels in the soil mass.

Plasticity : The property of soil, which allows it to be deformed beyond the point of recovery without cracking or appreciable volume change.

Plasticity Index, I_p (D) : Numerical difference between the liquid limit and the plastic limit.

Plastic Limit, w_p (D) : The water content, expressed as a percentage of weight of oven dry soil, at the boundary between the plastic and the semi-solid states of consistency of the soil.

Pore Pressure Coefficients (D) : The change in pore pressure due to change in applied stresses is expressed in terms of empirical coefficients known as pore pressure coefficients.

Porosity, n (D) : The ratio, usually expressed as a percentage, of the volume of voids of a given soil mass, to the total volume of the soil mass.

Preconsolidation Pressure (Prestress), p_o (FL^{-2}) : The maximum effective pressure to which a soil has been subjected.

Pressure Bulb : The zone in a loaded soil mass bounded by an arbitrarily selected isobar of stress.

Principal plane : Each of three mutually perpendicular planes through a point in a soil mass on which the shearing stress is zero.

Quick Condition (Quick sand) : Condition in which water is flowing upwards with sufficient velocity to reduce the shear resistance of the soil through a decrease in inter-granular pressure.

Relative Density : See 'Density Index.'

Remoulded : Soil that has had its natural structure modified by manipulation.

Rock : Natural solid mineral matter connected by strong and permanent cohesive forces, occurring in large masses of fragments.

Sand : Cohesionless aggregates of angular, sub-rounded, rounded, flaky or flat fragments of more or less unaltered rocks, or mineral of size between 4.75 mm and 75 microns.

Seepage (Percolation) : Slow movement of gravitational water through the soil.

Sensitivity : The ratio of unconfined comperssive strength of an undistrubed specimen, of the soil mass, to the unconfined compressive strength of specimen of the same soil after remoulding at unaltered water content. The effect of remoulding on the consistency of a cohesive soil.

Shear Failure (Failure by Rupture) : Failure in which movement caused by shearing stresses in a soil mass is of sufficient magnitude to destroy or seriously endanger a structure.

General Shear Failure : Failure in which the ultimate strength of the soil is mobilized along the entire potential surface of sliding.

Local Shear Failure : Failure in which the ultimate shearing strength of the soil is mobilized only locally along the potential surface of sliding.

Shear Strength, s (FL^{-2}) : The maximum resistance of a soil to shearing stresses.

Shrinkage Index, I_s (D) : The numerical difference between the plastic and shrinkage limit.

Shrinkage Limit w_s (D) : The maximum water content expressed as percentage of oven-dry weight at which any further reduction in water content will not cause a decrease in volume of the soil mass, the soil mass being initially of soil in its undisturbed state.

Silt : Fine grained soil which exhibits a little or no plasticity and has a little or no strength when air-dried.

Silt Size : The portion of a soil finer than 75-micron IS Sieve and coarser than 0.002 mm.

Skin Friction, ϕ (FL^{-2}) : The frictional resistance developed between soil and structure.

Soil (Earth) : Sediments or other unconsolidated accumulations of solid particles produced by the physical and chemical disintegration of rocks, and which may or may not contain organic matter.

Soil Mechanics : That branch of engineering which deals with the application of soil science, the static and dynamic laws and principles of mechanics and hydraulics to engineering problems dealing with soil as structural material.

Soil Profile (Profile) : Vertical section of soil, showing the natural and sequence of the various layers, as developed by deposition or weathering, or both.

Soil Stabilization : Chemical or mechanical treatment design to increase or maintain the stability of a mass of soil or otherwise to improve its engineering properties.

Soil Structure : Arrangement of soil particles in soil mass.

Flocculent Structure : An arrangement composed of flocs of soil particles instead of individual soil particles.

Honeycomb Structure : An arrangement composed of soil particles having a comparatively loose, stable structure resembling a honeycomb.

Single : Grained Structure : An arrangement composed of individual soil particles, characteristic structure of coarse-grained soils.

Stability Number, N_s (D) : A pure number used in the analysis of the stability of a soil embankment, defined by the following equation

$$N_s = c_d/(\gamma_c H_c)$$

where

c_d = mobilized cohesion,

γ_c = effective unit weight, and

H_c = critical height of the sloped bank.

Stability Factor (D) : It is the reciprocal of the stability number.

Standard Penetration Resistance : Number of blows required for 30 cm penetration of a standard sampling spoon with 65 kg hammer falling freely through a height of 75cm.

Subgrade : The soil prepared and compacted to support the pavement system.

Time Factor, T_v, T(D) : Dimensionless factor, utilized in the theory of consolidation, containing the physical constants of a soil stratum influencing its time-rate of consolidation, expressed as follows:

$$T = k(1 + e)/(a_v \gamma_w H^2) = c_v t/(H^2)$$

where

k = coefficient of permeability (LT^{-1})

e = void ratio (D)

t = elapsed time that the stratum has been consolidated (T)

a_v = coefficient of compressibility (L^2F^{-1});

γ_w = unit weight of water (FL^{-3})

c_v = coefficient of consolidation (L^2T^{-1}); and

H = thickness of stratum drained on one side only. If stratum is drained on both sides, its thickness equal 2H (L).

Toughness Index, I_T (D) : The ratio of the plasticity index to the flow index.

Triaxial Shear Test (Triaxial Compression Test) : A test in which a cylindrical specimen of soil encased in an impervious membrane is subjected to a confining pressure and then loaded axially to failure.

Ultimate Bearing Capacity (Gross), q_o (gross), q_{ult}(gross) (FL^{-2}) : The gross intensity of loading at the base of a foundation which causes shear failure of the soil support.

Ultimate Bearing Capacity (Nett), q_o (nett), q_{ult}(nett) (FL^{-2}) : The nett intensity of loading at the base of a foundation which causes shear failure of the soil support, in excess of that at the same level due to the surrounding surcharge, that is, ultimate bearing capacity (gross) minus the surcharge.

Unconfined Compressive Strength, q_u (FL^{-2}) : The load per unit area at which an unconfined prismatic or cylindrical specimen of standard dimensions of a soil will fail in a simple compression test.

Unconsolidated : Undrained Test (quick Test) : A soil test in which the water content of the test specimen remains practically unchanged during the application of the confining pressure and the additional axial (or shearing force)

Under-Consolidated Soil Deposit : A deposit that is not fully consolidated under the existing effective overburden pressure.

Undisturbed Sample : A soil sample that has been obtained by methods in which every precaution has been taken to minimize disturbance to the sample.

Unit Weight, γ (FL^{-3}) : Weight per unit volume of a soil mass.

Dry Unit weight, γ_d (FL^{-3}) : The weight of oven dry soil per unit of total volume of soil mass.

Effective Unit weight, γ_e (FL^{-3}) : That unit weight of a soil which, when multiplied by the height of the overlying column of soil, yields the effective pressure due to the weight of the overburden.

Saturated Unit weight, γ_{sat} (FL^{-3}) : The unit weight of soil mass when saturated.

Submerged Unit weight, γ_{sub} (FL^{-3}) : The weight of the solids in air minus the weight of water displaced by the solids per unit volume of soil mass; the saturated unit weight minus the unit weight of water.

Wet Unit weight, γ_{wet} (FL^{-3}) : The weight per unit of total volume of soil mass, irrespective of the degree of saturation.

Void : Space in a soil mass not occupied by solid mineral matter. This space may be occupied by air, water, or other gaseous or liquid material.

Void ratio, e (D) : The ratio of the volume of void space to the volume of solid particles in a given soil mass.

Critical void ratio, e_c (D) : The void ratio prior to the process of shear in which the net volume change at failure is zero.

Wall friction (FL^{-2}) : Frictional resistance mobilized between a wall and the soil in contact with the wall.

Water Holding Capacity (D) : The smallest value to which the water content of a soil can be reduced by gravity drainage.

Zero Air Void Curve (Saturation Curve) : Dry density moisture content curve for 100 percent saturation.

4

DETERMINATION OF MOISTURE CONTENT

4.1 AIM

To determine the moisture content of soil.

4.2 THEORY AND APPLICATIONS

Soil mass is a 3-phase system; consisting of solids, liquids and gaseous matter. The solids enclose water or air, wholly or partially. The open space between the solid particles is known as voids or pores. If voids are fully filled with air, the soil is called dry soil. When the voids in the soil are completely filled with water, the soil is said to be in saturated state or it is known as saturated soil. If the voids in a soil is partially filled with water and partly by air, the soil is called partially saturated or simply wet soil.

Moisture content (some times known as water content) of a soil is the ratio of the weight of water to the weight of solids, denoted as m and is given by the equation.

$$m = W_w / W_s$$

where

m = moisture content

W_w = weight of water

W_s = weight of solids.

Sometimes, for convenience the moisture content is expressed as percentage, which is expressed as

$$\text{Moisture content (\%)} = m \times 100.$$

In soil mechanics, moisture content assumes a very important role. The behaviour of soil depends significantly on its moisture content. Particularly moisture content plays an important role in understanding the behaviour of fine-grained soils. It is the moisture content which changes the soil from liquid state to plastic and solid state. The moisture content of a soil controls the shear strength and compressibility of soil. Compaction of soil in the field is also controlled by the quantity of water available in the soil during compaction. Because of this, the optimum moisture content of soil is estimated to use during compaction. Further, unit weight of soil is directly proportional to the moisture content. Density of soils is used in calculating the stability of slopes, bearing capacity of soil for foundation and earth pressure behind a retaining wall. The knowledge of determining the moisture content is required in many of the laboratory tests explained in this book.

4.3 APPARATUS

1. containers (Bins)
2. sensitive balance (least count 0.1g)
3. oven
4. desicator
5. Tongs (one pair)

4.4 PROCEDURE

1. Note the identification number marked on the bin.
2. Clean a bin along with its lid, dry and weigh (W_1)
3. Take the required quantity (50-100g–large quantity for coarse grained soil and small quantity for fine grained soil) of representative soil specimen into the bin and weigh the bin with the wet soil with lid (W_2)
4. Keep the container in the oven with the lid open, (it is a general practice to keep the lid at the base of the bin) dry the sample in the oven till its mass become constant (i.e. approximately for 24 hours)
5. Maintain the temperature of the oven between 105°C and 110°C for normal soils and 60°C to 80°C for soils having organic matter.

6. After drying, take out the bin from the oven and place it with lid in a desicator to cool down the sample without absorbing the humidity from the atmosphere.
7. Weigh the bin with lid along with the oven dry soil (W_1)
8. To obtain an average value take three trial using three bins simultaneously.
9. Enter the observations in Table 4.1

4.5 PRECAUTIONS

The following precautions need to be taken while performing the experiment.

1. The soil should be loosely placed in the bin, so as to allow easy evaporation of moisture.
2. Over heating should be avoided.
3. Ovendry soil should not be kept open to the atmosphere (for cooling) as it may absorb moisture from atmosphere.
4. Microwave oven may be used to dry the soil quickly to gain the time in situations such as student examinations. However, microwave oven dried soil cannot be used to perform any other tests such as Atterberg limits etc. This is because; the microwave oven dried soil will undergo changes in its structure and to some extent in its composition.
5. Ensure the identification number on the base and the lid of the bin is same.

4.6 CALCULATIONS

Moisture content m = weight of water /weight of solids.

But, weight of oven dry soil = weight of solids

Therefore m = weight of water/weight of dry soil

$$= (W_2 - W_3)/(W_3 - W_1)$$

m in (%) = m × 100

where

W_1 = weight of container with lid

W_2 = weight of container with lid + wet soil

W_3 = weight of container with lid + dry soil

4.7 OBSERVATIONS

TABLE 4.1
OBSERVATIONS FOR MOISTURE CONTENT DETERMINATIONS

Project name & location of site:

Project report No:

Location of sample:

Sample collected on: Sample collected by:

Sample tested on: Sample tested by:

Trial Number	1	2	3
1. Bin identification number			
2. Mass of empty bin W_1, (g)			
3. Mass of bin + wet soil W_2, (g)			
4. Mass of bin + dry soil W_3, (g)			
5. Mass of water (3) - (4) , (g)			
6. Mass of solids (4) - (2) , (g)			
7. Moisture content, m = (5)/(6)			
8. m in (%) = (7) × 100			

4.8 RESULT

Average moisture content (m) =

4.9 QUESTIONS

1. What is the difference between the air-dried and oven dried soil sample?
2. Why do you dry the soil sample at a temperature less than 110°C? Why not at a higher temperature?
3. What are the practical applications of moisture content in the field?
4. Why does the quantity of soil taken for determination of moisture content depends upon the particle size? (more quantity for coarse grained soil and less quantity for fine particles).
5. What are free pore water and water of hydration? Which one do you determine in this test? Explain.

5

DETERMINATION OF SPECIFIC GRAVITY OF SOIL SOLIDS

AIM

To determine specific gravity of soil solids

THEORY AND APPLICATION

Specific gravity of soil solids is the ratio of weight, in air of a given volume, of dry soil solids to the weight of equal volume of water at 4°C. Specific gravity of soil grains gives the property of the formation of soil mass and is independent of particle size. Specific gravity of soil grains is used in calculating void ratio, porosity and degree of saturation, by knowing moisture content and density using the following relationship.

$$\gamma = (eS + Gs)\,\gamma_w/(1 + e)$$

$$m = (eS/G_s)$$

where

γ = unit weight of soil (unless specified, unit weight refers to wet unit weight)

e = void ratio

S = degree of saturation (ratio)

G_s = specific gravity of soil solids

γ_w = unit weight of water

m = moisture content in ratio.

The value of specific gravity helps in identifying and classifying the soil type. It gives an idea about the suitability of the soil as a construction material. Higher value of specific gravity indicates more compactness and gives more strength for roads and foundations. It is also used in estimating the critical hydraulic gradient in soil when a sand boiling condition is being studied and in zero air-void calculations in the compaction theory of soils. The general range of specific gravity values for different soils is

Metal oar ≥ 3

Coarse grained soils 2.6-2.7

Fine grained soils 2.7-2.8

Organic soils 2.3 -2.5

APPARATUS

1. Pycnometer (for coarse grained soil) or specific gravity bottle (for fine grained soil)
2. 4.75 mm sieve
3. vacuum pump (or hot water bath)
4. weighing balance
5. oven
6. dessicator
7. glass rod
8. distilled water

PROCEDURE

The procedure presented below is for coarse-grained soil. However, the same procedure is followed for fine-grained soil but read pycnometer as specific gravity bottle in case of fine-grained soil.

1. Dry the pycnometer (specific gravity bottle for fine grained soil) and weigh it with its cap (W_1)
2. Take about 200g (about 50g for fine grained soil) of oven dried soil passing through 4.75mm sieve into the pycnometer (specimen containing natural moisture content may also be taken, but oven dry mass of the soil must be determined at the end of the test) and weigh again (W_2)

3. Add sufficient de-aired water to cover the soil and screw on the cap.
4. Shake the pycnometer well and connect it to the vacuum pump to remove entrapped air for about 10 minutes.
5. After the air has been removed, fill the pycnometer with water completely.
6. Thoroughly dry the pycnometer from out side and weigh it (W_3)
7. Clean the pycnometer by washing thoroughly.
8. Fill the cleaned pycnometer completely with water upto its top with cap screw on.
9. Weigh the pycnometer after drying it on the outside thoroughly (W_4)
10. Repeat the test to complete three trials and to obtain an average value of specific gravity.

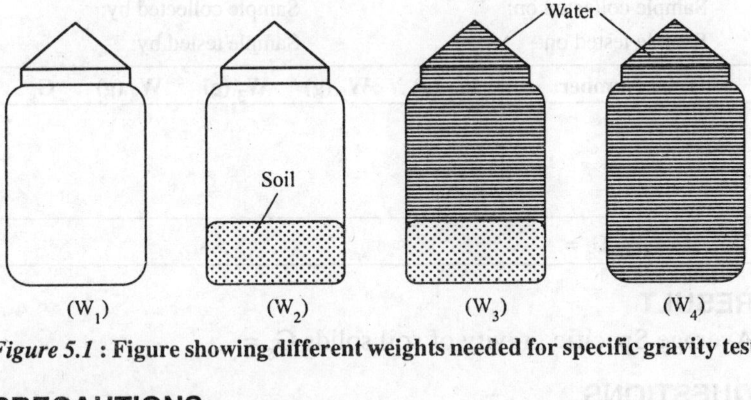

Figure 5.1 **: Figure showing different weights needed for specific gravity test**

PRECAUTIONS

1. Soil grains whose specific gravity is to be determined should be completely dry.
2. Dried soil taken for testing should have the soil grain of its original size. If on drying soil lumps are formed, they should be broken to its original size.
3. Inaccuracies in weighing and failure to completely eliminate the entrapped air are the main sources of error. Both should be avoided by careful working.

OBSERVATIONS AND CALCULATIONS

Determine the specific gravity of soil grains (G_s) using the following equation.

$$G_s = (W_2 - W_1)/\{(W_2 - W_1) - (W_3 - W_4)\}$$

where

W_1 = empty weight of pycnometer

W_2 = weight of pycnometer + oven dry soil

W_3 = weight of pycnometer + oven dry soil + water

W_4 = weight of pycnometer + water full

TABLE 5.1
OBSERVATIONS FOR SPECIFIC GRAVITY DETERMINATION

Project name & location of site:

Project report No:

Location of sample:

Sample collected on: Sample collected by:

Sample tested on: Sample tested by:

Trial Number	W_1 (g)	W_2 (g)	W_3 (g)	W_4 (g)	G_s
1					
2					
3					
Average G_s =					

RESULT

Average Specific gravity of soil solids G_s =

QUESTIONS

1. What is the difference between the specific gravity of soil grains and soil?
2. What are normal ranges of specific gravity of gravel, clay and organic soils?
3. What are the units of specific gravity of soil grains in MKS system?
4. What are the field applications of specific gravity of soil grains?

5. If a liquid other than water is used in the specific gravity experiment, what modifications in the expression of specific gravity are to be made?
6. During the test, if air is not completely removed, what is the effect on the value of specific gravity?
7. If the soil taken for test is not completely dry, what is the effect on the value of specific gravity?
8. If a coarse grained soil is crushed to powder, what happens to its specific gravity value? Why?
9. Draw the phase diagram for a wet soil.
10. What is the need of having a conical cap for the pycnometer?

6

DETERMINATION OF FIELD DENSITY (UNIT WEIGHT) OF SOIL BY CORE CUTTER METHOD

AIM

To determine the field density of soil by core cutter method.

THEORY AND APPLICATIONS

Density (or unit weight) is defined as the weight per unit volume.

$$\text{Unit weight } \gamma = W/V$$

where

γ = unit weight of soil

W = weight of soil

V = volume of soil

Here, weight and volume of soil comprise the whole soil mass. The voids in the soil may be filled with both water and air or only air or only water consequently the soil may be wet, dry or saturated. In soils the weight of air is considered negligible and therefore the saturated unit weight is maximum, dry unit weight is minimum and wet unit weight is in between the two. If soils are below water table, submerged unit weight is also estimated. The unit weight is expressed as g/cm^3 or t/m^3 or kg/m^3 or lb/ft^3.

Unit weight of soil reflects the strength of soil against compression and shear. Unit weight of soil is used in calculating the stresses in the soil due to its overburden pressure. It is useful in estimating bearing capacity and settlement of foundations. Earth pressure behind the retaining walls and in cuts is checked with the help of unit weight of the associated soils. It is the unit weight of the soil, which controls the field compaction and it helps in the design of embankment slopes. Permeability of soil depends on its unit weight. It may be noted here that, field density always refers to dry unit weight because the wet unit weight of soil at location varies from season to season and based on the fluctuations of the local water table level and surface water.

APPARATUS

1. Cylindrical core cutter
2. Steel rammer
3. Steel dolly
4. Balance
5. Steel rule
6. Spade or pickaxe
7. Straight edge
8. Knife
9. Bins for water content
10. Dessicator
11. Oven
12. Tongs.

PROCEDURE

1. Measure the height (h) and internal diameter (d) of the core cutter and apply grease to the inside of the core cutter.
2. Weigh the empty core cutter (W_1).
3. Clean and level the place where density is to be determined.
4. Drive the core cutter, with a steel dolly on its top as shown in Fig. 6.1, into the soil to its full depth with the help of a steel rammer.

5. Excavate the soil around the cutter with a crow bar and gently lift the cutter without disturbing the soil in it.
6. Trim the top and bottom surfaces of the sample and clean the outside surface of the cutter.
7. Weigh the core cutter with soil (W_2).
8. Remove the soil from the core cutter, using a sample ejector, and take a representative soil sample from it to determine the moisture content (m). The procedure for the determination of moisture content is explained in Chapter Four.

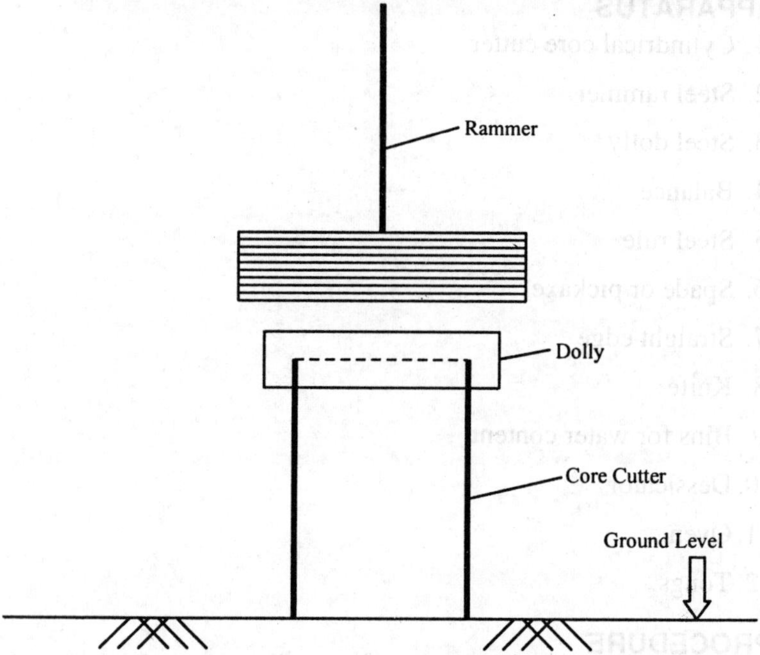

Figure 6.1 **: Core cutter test apparatus**

PRECAUTIONS

1. Core cutter method of determining the field density of soil is only suitable for fine grained soil (Silts and clay). This is because collection of undisturbed soil sample from a coarse grained soil is difficult and hence the field properties, including unit weight, cannot be maintained in a core sample.

2. Core cutter should be driven into the ground till the steel dolly penetrates into the ground half way only so as to avoid compaction of the soil in the core.
3. Before lifting the core cutter, soil around the cutter should be removed to minimise the disturbance.

OBSERVATIONS AND CALCULATIONS

1. Enter all the observations in Table 6.1
2. Calculate wet (γ_{wet}) unit weight of the soil using the following relationship

$$\gamma_{wet} = (W_2 - W_1)/V$$

where

W_1 = empty weight of core cutter

W_2 = weight of core cutter + soil

V = volume of core cutter ($\pi d^2 h/4$)

d = inner diameter of core cutter

h = height of core cutter

3. Calculate dry unit weight. $\gamma_{dry} = \gamma_{wet} / (1+ m)$
4. Calculate void ratio (e), porosity (n) and degree of saturation(S).

TABLE 6.1

Observations to determine the physical properties of soil by core cutter method

Project name & location of site:

Project report No:

Location of sample:

Sample collected by: Sample collected on:

Sample tested by: Sample tested on:

Internal diameter of core cutter (d) =

Height of core cutter (h)=

Volume of the core cutter (V) ($V = \pi d^2 h/4$) =

Specific gravity of soil solids (G_s) =

Trial Number	1	2	3
1. Weight of core cutter, W_1 (g)			
2. Weight of core cutter + soil W_2 (g)			
3. Weight of wet soil, $(W_2 - W_1)$ (g)			
4. Wet unit weight of soil, $\gamma_{wet} = (W_2 - W_1)/V$ (g/cm^3)			
Moisture content Calculations			
5. Bin identification Number			
6. Empty weight of bin (g)			
7. Weight of bin +wet soil (g)			
8. Weight of bin + dry soil (g)			
9. Weight of water (7) – (8) (g)			
10. Weight of dry soil (8) – (6) (g)			
11. Moisture content, m (9)/(10)			
12. Dry unit weight $\gamma_{dry} = \gamma_{wet}/(1 + m)$ (γ/cm^3)			
13. Void ratio, $e = (G_s \gamma_w/\gamma_{dry}) - 1$			
14. Degree of saturation, $S = mG_s/e$			

RESULT

Wet unit weight of soil =

Dry Unit weight =

Moisture content =

Degree of saturation =

Void ratio =

QUESTIONS

1. What do you understand by dry, wet, saturated and submerged unit weights of soil? Explain.
2. Out of various types of densities, which one of them is maximum and which is minimum? Explain.
3. If you know dry unit weights, moisture content and specific gravity of a soil, how do you calculate its wet, saturated and submerged densities?
4. Differentiate between unit weight, relative density and specific gravity of a soil.

5. What are the field problems, where density of soil need to be determined?
6. Why do you stop driving the core cutter as soon as it get completely driven and only part of the dolly is driven? Why not till the complete dolly is driven into the ground? Explain.
7. In what type of soils do we prefer core cutter method of determining the field density? Why?
8. In fully saturated soils, what is the degree of saturation?
9. What is the degree of saturation in oven dry soils?

7

DETERMINATION OF FIELD DENSITY (UNIT WEIGHT) OF SOIL BY SAND REPLACEMENT METHOD

AIM

To determine the field density of soil at a given location by sand replacement method.

APPARATUS

1. Sand pouring cylinder (SPC)
2. Calibrating can
3. Metal tray with a central hole
4. Dry sand (passing through 600 micron sieve)
5. Balance
6. Moisture content bins
7. Oven
8. Desiccator
9. Glass plate (about 45 cm square)
10. Metal tray
11. Scraper tool.

THEORY AND APPLICATIONS

In core cutter method, explained in Chapter Six, the unit weight of soil is obtained from direct measurement of weight and volume of soil obtained from field. However, it is always (particularly in sandy soils) not possible to obtain a core sample. In such situations, the sand replacement method is employed to determine the unit weight. In sand replacement method, a small cylindrical pit is excavated and the weight of the soil excavated from the pit is measured. A sand whose density is known is filled into the pit. By measuring the weight of sand required to fill the pit and knowing its density the volume of pit is calculated. Knowing the weight of soil excavated from the pit and the volume of pit the density of soil is calculated. Therefore, in this experiment there are two stages. (1) Calibration of sand density and (2) Measurement of soil density. The practical applications of unit weight of soil is already discussed in Chapter Six.

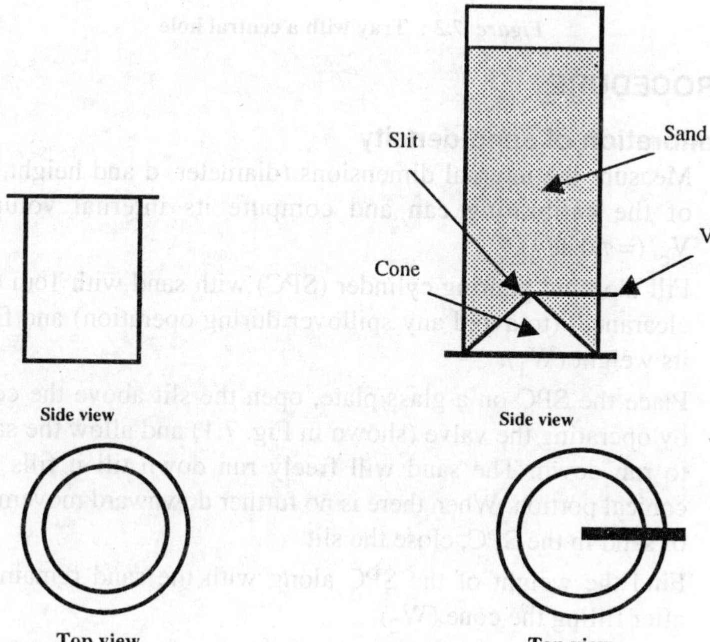

(*a*) Calibrating can **(*b*) Sand pouring cylinder (SPC)**

***Figure 7.1*: Calibrating can and sand pouring cylinder**

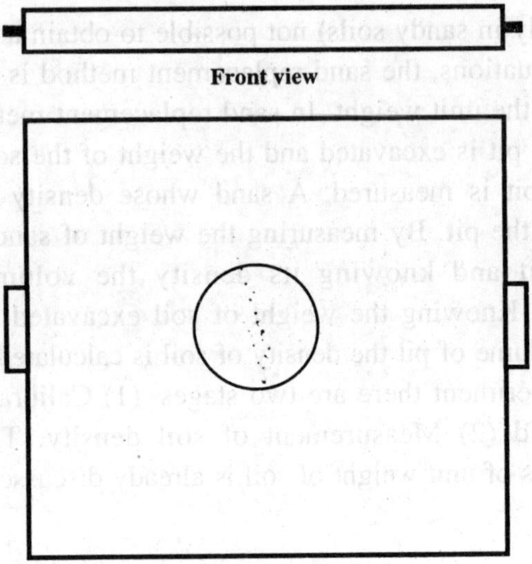

Figure 7.2 : **Tray with a central hole**

PROCEDURE

Calibration of sand density

1. Measure the internal dimensions (diameter, d and height, h) of the calibrating can and compute its internal volume V_c, $(= \pi d^2 h/4)$.
2. Fill the sand pouring cylinder (SPC) with sand with 1cm top clearance (to avoid any spillover during operation) and find its weight (W_1).
3. Place the SPC on a glass plate, open the slit above the cone by operating the valve (shown in Fig. 7.1) and allow the sand to run down. The sand will freely run down till it fills the conical portion. When there is no further downward movement of sand in the SPC, close the slit.
4. Find the weight of the SPC along with the sand remaining after filling the cone (W_2).
5. Place the SPC concentrically on top of the calibrating can. Open the slit to allow the sand to run down until the sand flow stops by itself. This operation will fill the calibrating can and the

conical portion of the SPC. Now close the slit and find the weight of the SPC with the remaining sand (W_3).

MEASUREMENT OF SOIL DENSITY

1. Clean and level the ground surface where the field density is to be determined.
2. Place the tray with a central hole over the portion of the soil to be tested.
3. Excavate a pit into the ground, through the hole in the plate, approximately 12 cm deep (close the height of the calibrating can). The hole in the tray will guide the diameter of the pit to be made in the ground.
4. Collect the excavated soil into the tray and weigh the soil (W).
5. Determine the moisture content of the excavated soil as explained in Chapter 4.
6. Place the SPC, with sand having the latest weight of W_3, over the pit so that the base of the cylinder covers the pit concentrically.
7. Open the slit of the SPC and allow the sand to run into the pit freely, till there is no downward movement of sand level in the SPC and then close the slit.
8. Find the weight of the SPC with the remaining sand (W_4).

PRECAUTIONS

1. If for any reason it is necessary to excavate the pit to a depth other than 12 cm, the standard calibrating can should be replaced by one with an internal height same as the depth of pit to be made in the ground.
2. Care should be taken in excavating the pit, so that it is not enlarged by levering, as this will result in lower density being recorded.
3. No loose material should be left in the pit.
4. There should be no vibrations during this test.
5. It should not be forgotten to remove the tray, before placing the SPC over the pit.

OBSERVATIONS AND CALCULATIONS

1. Enter all the readings in Tables 7.1 and 7.2.
2. Unit weight of sand (γ_{sand}) is calculated as shown in Table 7.1. This is used in determining the volume of the pit made in the soil.
3. Table 7.2 shows the calculation of wet, dry unit weight, void ratio and degree of saturation of the soil.

TABLE 7.1

Calibration of unit weight of sand

Trial No.	1	2
1. Volume of the calibrating container, V (cc)		
2. Weight of SPC + sand, W_1 (g)		
3. Weight of SPC + sand, W_2 (g) (after filling conical portion on a flat surface)		
4. Weight of SPC + sand, W_3 (g) (after filling calibrating can)		
5. Weight of sand required to fill cone, $W_c = W_1 - W_2$ (g)		
6. Weight of sand required to fill cone and can, $W_{cc} = W_2 - W_3$(g)		
7. Weight of sand in calibrating can = $W_{cc} - W_c$ (g)		
8. Unit weight of sand, $\gamma_{sand} = (W_{cc} - W_c)/V$ (g/cc)		

TABLE 7.2

Determination of unit weight of soil

Specific gravity of soil solids (given) G_s =

Trial No.	1	2	3
1. Weight of SPC after filling the hole & Conical portion, W_4 (g)			
2. Weight of sand in the hole and cone($W_3 - W_4$) (g)			
3. Weight of sand in the pit $W_p = (W_3 - W_4) - W_c$ (Table 7.1) (g)			
4. Volume of sand required to fill the pit $V_p = W_p / \gamma_{sand}$ (cc)			
5. Weight of the soil excavated from the pit (W) (g)			
6. Wet unit weight of the soil $\gamma_{wet} = W/V_p$ (g/cc)			
7. Dry unit weight of the soil $\gamma_{dry} = \gamma_{wet}/(1 + m)$ (g/cc)			
8. Void ratio of soil (e) $= \gamma_w G_s/(\gamma_{dry}) - 1$			
9. Degree of saturation (S) $= mG_s/e$			

RESULTS

1. Wet unit weight of soil =
2. Dry unit weight of soil =
3. Moisture content =
4. Degree of saturation =
5. Void ratio =

QUESTIONS

1. Why do you prefer to keep the depth of the hole equal to the height of the calibrating cylinder?
2. What is the necessity of the conical portion at the bottom of the SPC? What happens if it is not there?
3. In what type of soils is the sand replacement method of determining the field density is preferred? Why?
4. What should be the approximate angle of the cone?
5. In field densities, why do we give importance to dry density than wet density?
6. In sand replacement method, while filling the pit with sand, what happens to the results if the SPC is kept over the metal tray?

8

DETERMINATION OF GRAIN SIZE DISTRIBUTION OF SOIL BY SIEVE ANALYSIS

AIM

To conduct sieve analysis of soil to classify the given coarse-grained soil.

THEORY AND APPLICATION

Grain-size analysis is used in the engineering classification of soils. Particularly coarse grained soils. Part of the suitability criteria of soils for road, airfield, levee, dam and other embankment construction is the grain size analysis. Information obtained from the grain size analysis can be used to predict soil-water movement, although the permeability tests are more generally used. The suitability of frost action in soil, an extremely important consideration in colder climates, can be predicted from the grain size analysis. Soils are broadly classified as coarse-grained soils (gravel and sand) and fine grained soils (silt and clay). Further classification of coarse-grained soils depends mainly on grain-size distribution and the fine-grained soils are further classified based on their plasticity properties. The grain size distribution of coarse-grained soil is studied by conducting sieve analysis and the hydrometer analysis is used to study the grain size distribution of fine-grained soils.

As per IS classification of soils:

Soils are classified as coarse grained and fine-grained soils.

Coarse grained soils

Soils having particles coarser then 0.075 mm size is termed as coarse grained soils. There are various grain size classifications in use. The more commonly used systems are (*i*) U.S. Bureau of soil and Public Road Administration (PRA) system, (*ii*) International soil classification, (*ii*) The Massachusetts Institute of Technology (M.I.T.) classification and (*iii*) Indian Standard (IS: 1498) classification. The details of each of the above methods are consolidated below.

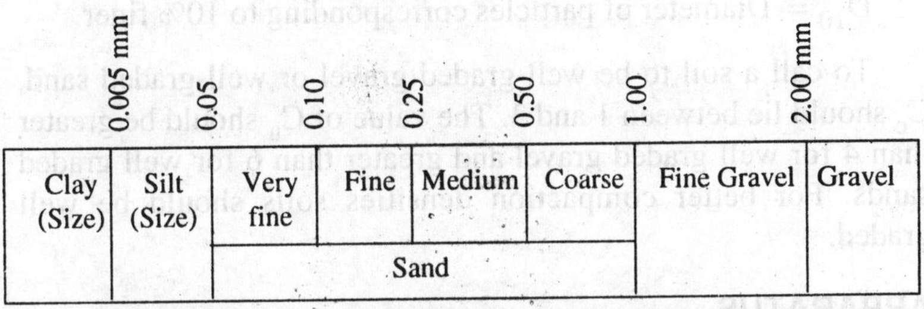

Figure 8.1(a) **: U.S. Bureau of Soils and PRA Classification**

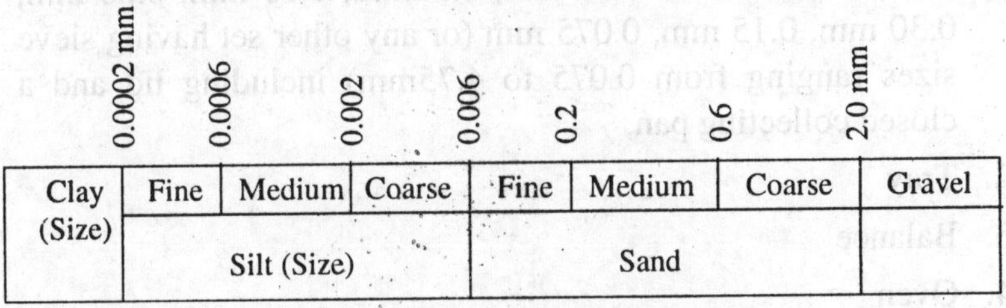

Figure 8.1(b) **: M.I.T. Classification**

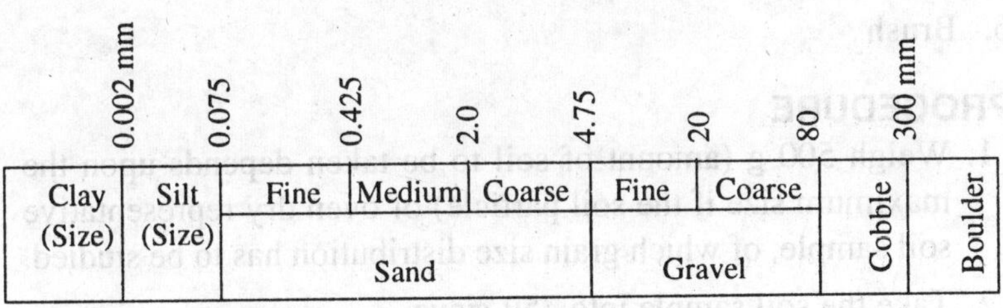

Figure 8-1(c) **: Indian standard classification**

Besides the particle size, the distribution of different sizes is needed to classify the soil as either well graded or poorly graded.

The two parameters (i.e. Uniformity coefficient C_u and coefficient of curvature C_c) obtained from the grain size analysis tests are utilised in the classification of soil.

$$\text{Uniformity coefficient } (C_u) = D_{60}/D_{10} \quad (8.1)$$

$$\text{Coefficient of curvature } (C_c) = (D_{30})^2/(D_{60} \times D_{10}) \quad (8.2)$$

where

D_{60} = Diameter of particles corresponding to 60% finer.

D_{30} = Diameter of particles corresponding to 30% finer.

D_{10} = Diameter of particles corresponding to 10% finer.

To call a soil to be well-graded gravel or well-graded sand, C_c should lie between 1 and 3. The value of C_u should be greater than 4 for well graded gravel and greater than 6 for well graded sands. For better compaction densities soils should be well graded.

APPARATUS

1. A sieve set of size 4.75 mm, 2.36mm, 1.18 mm, 0.60 mm, 0.30 mm, 0.15 mm, 0.075 mm (or any other set having sieve sizes ranging from 0.075 to 4.75mm) including lid and a closed collecting pan.
2. Tray
3. Balance
4. Oven
5. Sieve shaker
6. Brush

PROCEDURE

1. Weigh 500 g (amount of soil to be taken depends upon the maximum size if the soil particle) of oven dry representative soil sample, of which grain size distribution has to be studied.
2. Take the soil sample into 75μ sieve.
3. Wash the soil sample keeping it in the sieve. Washing of soil sample means: place the soil in the sieve and gently

pour water over the soil so that it wets the soil and remove the fine particles (clay & silt particles) in the form of mud, leaving only the sand and gravel size particles in the sieve.

4. Transfer the soil retained in the sieve, after washing, into a tray. Invert the sieve into the tray and pour water gently so that all the soil particles retained in the sieve are transferred into the tray.
5. Keep the tray in the oven for 24 hours at 105°C to dry it completely.
6. Weigh the oven dry soil in the tray (W_o).
7. The weight of the fine grained soil (silt and clay) is equal to $500 - W_o$.
8. Clean the sieve set so that no soil particles were struck in them (during earlier tests).
9. Arrange the sieves in order such that coarse sieve is kept at the top and the fine sieve is at the bottom. Place a closed pan below the finest sieve.
10. Take the oven-dried soil obtained after washing into the top sieve and keep the lid to close the top sieve.
11. Position the sieve set in the sieve shaker and sieve the sample for a period of 10 minutes.
12. Separate the sieves and weigh carefully the amount of soil retained on each sieve. This is usually done by transfering the soil retained on each seive on a separate piece of paper and weighing the soil with the paper.
13. Enter the observations in the Table 8.1 and calculate the cumulative percentage of soil retained on each sieve.
14. Draw the grain size distribution curve (also called gradation curve) between the grain size (on log scale) on the

X-axis and the percentage finer (on normal scale) on the Y-axis.

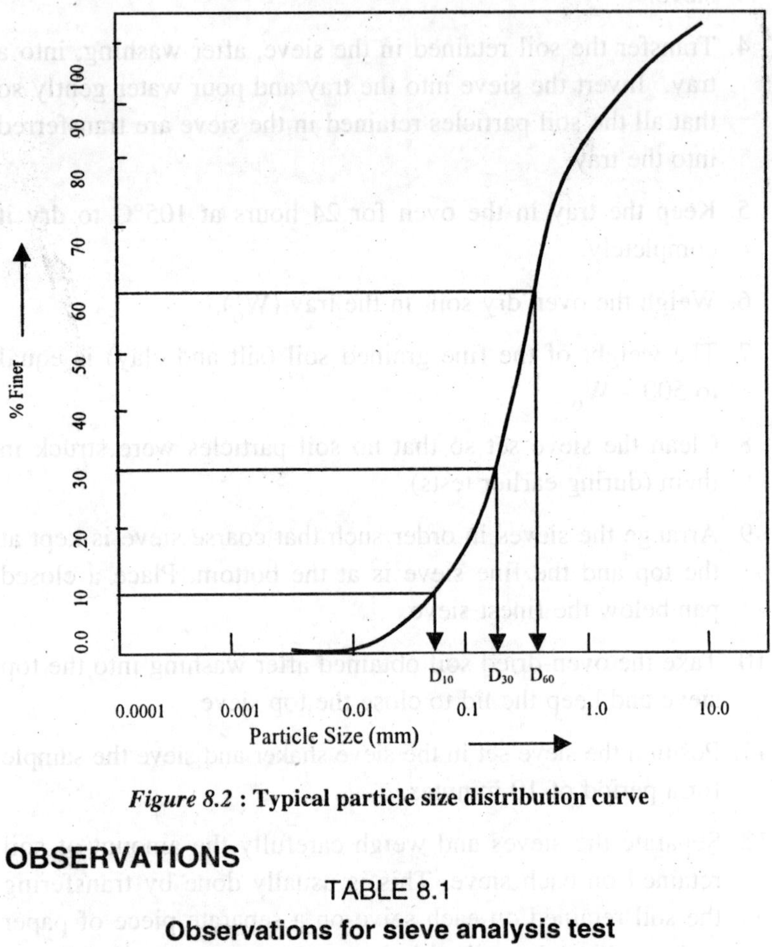

Figure 8.2 : **Typical particle size distribution curve**

OBSERVATIONS

TABLE 8.1
Observations for sieve analysis test

Project name & location of site:

Project report No:

Location of sample:

Sample collected on: Sample collected by:

Sample tested on: Sample tested by:

Weight of the soil taken for testing (W):

Aperture size of sieve (mm)	Wt. of soil retained (g) (Wr)	% Wt. retained $p_w = (W_r / W) \times 100$	Cumulative Wt. retained $C_p = \Sigma p_w$	% finer $100 - C_p$

CALCULATIONS

Plot a semi-log graph between percentage finer and logarithmic grain size (mm). From the graph, obtain the percentage of coarse, medium and fine sands. Also obtain

Uniformity coefficient (C_u) and coefficient of curvature (C_c) using Eqs. (8.1) and (8.2).

RESULTS

Percentage gravel (> 4.75 mm) =

Percentage coarse sand (4.75 – 2.00 mm) =

Percentage of medium sand (2.00 – 0.425 mm) =

Percentage of fine sand (0.425 – 0.075 mm) =

Percentage of fines (silts & clay < 0.075 mm) =

Uniformity coefficient C_u =

Coefficient of curvature C_c =

QUESTIONS

1. What is the purpose of sieve analysis?
2. Why do you classify the soil?
3. What are the coarse grained and fine grained soils as per Indian Standard (IS) classification?
4. Can you classify all types of soils by sieve analysis?
5. Why do you use semi-log graph paper for plotting the grain size distribution curve?
6. What do you understand by well-graded and uniformly graded soils?
7. Draw the grain size distribution curves for poorly graded, well-graded and uniformly graded soils.

8. What do you understand by GW, GP, GM, GC, SW, SP, SM, SC in soil classification?
9. What are the considerations to fix the quantity of soil to be taken for sieve analysis?
10. What is meant by a gap graded soil?
11. When do you use double symbol classification?
12. What is A-line and how do you obtain A-line?
13. How the clays and silts are classified?

9

DETERMINATION OF GRAIN SIZE DISTRIBUTION OF SOIL BY HYDROMETER ANALYSIS

AIM

To conduct hydrometer analysis of soil to study the grain size distribution of the fine grained soil.

APPARATUS AND MATERIALS

1. Hydrometer
2. Dispersion cup with mechanical stirrer with complete accessories.
3. Two glass jars of 1 litre capacity.
4. Deflocculating agent (Sodium hexa metaphosphate solution prepared by dissolving 33g of sodium hexa metaphosphate and 7g of sodium carbonate in distilled water to make one litre solution).
5. Stop watch.
6. Thermometer

PROCEDURE

(a) For soils containing considerable amount of fines

1. Take about 50g in case of clayey soils and 100g in case of sandy soil and weigh it correctly to 0.1g.
2. In case the soil contains considerable amount of organic

matter or calcium compounds, pre-treatment of the soil with Hydrogen Peroxide or Hydrochloric acid may be necessary. In case of soils containing less than 20 percent of the above substances pre-treatment shall be avoided.

3. To the soil thus treated, add 100cc of Sodium hexa metaphosphate solution and warm it gently for the 10minutes and transfer the contents to the cup of the mechanical mixer using a jet of distilled water to wash all traces of the soil.
4. Stir the soil suspension for about 15minutes.
5. Transfer the suspension to the Hydrometer jar and make up the volume exactly to 1000cc, by adding distilled water.
6. Take another Hydrometer jar with 1000cc distilled water to store the Hydrometer in between consecutive readings of the soil suspension to be recorded. Note the specific gravity (r_w) readings and the temperature T°C of the water occasionally.
7. Mix the soil suspension roughly, by placing the palm of the right hand over the open end and holding the bottom of the jar with the left hand turning the jar upside down and back. When the jar is upside down be sure no soil is stuck to the base of the graduated jar.
8. Immediately after shaking, place the Hydrometer jar on the table and start the stopwatch. Insert the Hydrometer into the suspension carefully (avoiding circular or vertical oscillations to facilitate quick and accurate reading of the Hydrometer) and take Hydrometer readings at the total elapsed times of ¼, ½, 1 and 2 minutes.
9. After the 2 minutes reading, remove the hydrometer and transfer it to the distilled water jar and repeat step No. 8. Normally a pair of the same readings should be obtained before proceeding further.
10. Take the subsequent Hydrometer readings at elapsed timings of 4, 9,16, 25, 36, 49, 60 minutes and every one hour there after. Each time a reading is taken remove the Hydrometer from the suspension and keep it in the jar containing distilled

water. Care should be taken when the Hydrometer recorded, to see that the Hydrometer is at rest without any movement. As time elapses, because of the fall of the solid particles the density of the fluid suspension decreases readings, which should be checked as a guard against possible error in readings of the Hydrometer.

11. Continue recording operation of the Hydrometer readings until the Hydrometer reads 1000 approximately.

(b) When the soil contains a small proportion of fines:

1. Conduct sieve analysis on the soil as explained in Chapter Eight.
2. Take 50 g of the soil passing 75μ sieve and run the Hydrometer analysis as explained above.

   The correction to be applied for the percentage finer in the combined analysis is explained under calculations.

(c) Calibration of the Hydrometer

1. Note the mid length of the bulb.
2. Note the distance Z_r (cm) from the first and the last readings and any intermediate readings also on the stem of the Hydrometer to the mid length of the bulb.
3. Plot a curve (A) between the Hydrometer reading R_h against depth (Z_r). This curve is applicable for readings obtained from the first two minutes with the Hydrometer continuously kept inside the Hydrometer jar. For all subsequent readings of the Hydrometer, a correction has to be applied by subtracting the volume effect of the Hydrometer from the observed values Z_r. The value of this correction is V_r 2A where V_r is the volume of the Hydrometer, which can be obtained from the volume it displaces when immersed in water (g). The area of cross section of the jar may be obtained by dividing the volume of the jar between two marks by the distance between them.
4. After determining the correction factor, plot a graph ordinate of curve A. This curve is used for all the readings beyond the first two minutes.

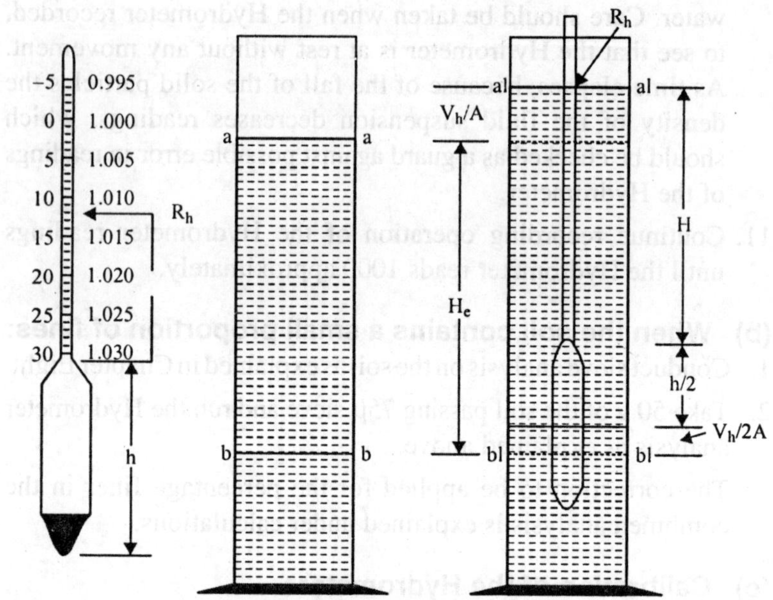

(a) Hydrometer (b) Sedimentation Jar before Immersion of Hydrometer (c) Effect of Hydrometer Immersion

Figure 9.1 **: Hydrometer Analysis**

CALCULATIONS

1. Diameter of the soil particles may be obtained from Stroke's law

$$D = \sqrt{30\eta} \times \sqrt{(Z_r/t)/(G - \gamma_w)}$$

Where D is the diameter of the soil particles (mm) Z_r is the depth of the immersion obtained from the calibration curve, (cm) t is the total elapsed time in minutes, η is the viscosity of the water at the temperature of the experiment in g-sec/cm² and γ_w is the unit weight of the water at the experiment temperature.

If the temperature during the experiment is constant, then the term within the bracket will be a constant and the above equation may be conveniently written as

$$D^2 = K Z_r / t$$

where

t = time in minutes

D = diameter of particle in mm

$K = 30\eta/(G - \gamma_w)$

2. The percentage finer N may be obtained from

$$N\% = GV/((G-1)xW) \times (r - r_w) \times 100$$

where

V = volume of soil suspension, (1000cc)

W = weight of dry soil taken for the test

r = hydrometer reading in distilled water

r_w = hydrometer readings in soil suspension.

G = specific gravity of soil particles.

Since V = 1000 cc, the above equation may be conveniently represented as follows:

$$N\% = K_1 (R_{h1} - 1000) \times 100$$

where

$K_1 = G/(G-1) \times (1000/W)$

R_{h1} = hydrometer reading $= R_h + C_m - C_d \pm C_t$

where

R_h = actually observed hydrometer reading (upper meniscus)

C_m = the meniscus correction

C_t = correction for temperature (positive if the test temperature is more than the temperature at which the hydrometer is calibrated and vice versa)

C_d = correction for the dispersing agent.

3. For the combined analysis, correction for the percentage finer is estimated as

$$N_c = N \times W_1/W_2$$

where

W_1 = weight of soil passing 75μ sieve

W_2 = total weight of dry soil used

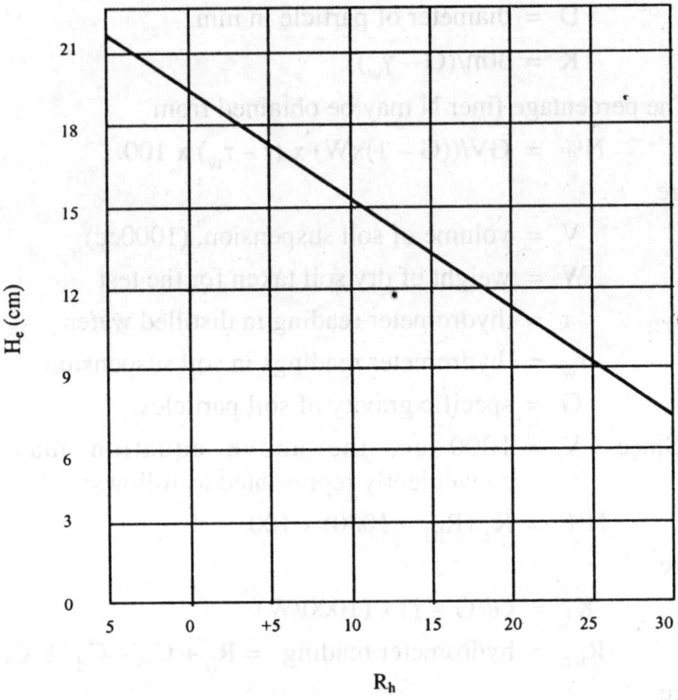

Figure 9.2 **: Typical calibration curve for the hydrometer**

TABLE 9.1

Specific gravity of distilled water

Temp °C	0	2	4	6	8
10	0.99973	0.99952	0.99927	0.99897	0.99862
20	0.99823	0.99780	0.99733	0.99681	0.99626
30	0.99568	0.9951	0.9944	0.9937	-

TABLE 9.2

Viscosity of water at different temperatures in milliposies

Temp °C	0	2	4	6	8
10	13.10	12.39	11.75	11.16	10.60
20	10.69	9.61	9.61	8.75	8.36
30	8.00	7.67	7.36	7.06	6.79

TABLE 9.3

Temperature correction (C_t) for hydrometer analysis

Temp in °C	Correction	Temp in °C	Correction
20.0	Nil	28.0	0.00178
20.5	0.00009	28.5	0.00191
21.0	0.00017	29.0	0.00206
21.5	0.00027	29.5	0.00219
22.0	0.00037	30.0	0.00232
22.5	0.00049	30.5	0.00247
23.0	0.00058	31.0	0.00262
23.5	0.00068	31.5	0.00278
24.0	0.00081	32.0	0.00291
24.5	0.00092	32.5	0.00320
25.0	0.00102	33.0	0.00350
25.5	0.00116	33.5	0.00380
26.0	0.00127	34.0	0.00400
26.5	0.00139	34.5	0.00420
27.0	0.00150	35.0	0.00470
27.5	0.00163	-	

QUESTIONS

1. What is Hydrometer analysis?
2. What is stroke's law? How does it help in hydrometer analysis?
3. What is Hydrometer calibration? Where is it used?
4. What does hydrometer measure?
5. What is meniscus correction? How do you determine it? What is its use?
6. What is the effect of the size of soil particles on their velocity in soil water suspension?
7. When do you go for hydrometer analysis?
8. How are the readings marked on a hydrometer?
9. What are the other corrections that are to be applied to the observed readings of the hydrometer?

10

DETERMINATION OF PERMEABILITY OF SOILS

AIM

To determine the coefficient of permeability of a given soil sample by conducting

1. Variable head test, and
2. Constant head test.

THEORY AND APPLICATIONS

The property of the soil which permits water (fluid) to percolate through its continuously connected voids is called its permeability (or hydraulic conductivity). In soil mechanics, the coefficient of permeability K expresses the degree of permeability. It has the velocity dimensions.

Factors effecting the coefficient of permeability can be studied from the equation

$$K = C\, d^2\, \gamma_w/\eta \;\; (e^3/(1+e)) \qquad (10.1)$$

where

K = coefficient of permeability

C = constant

d = average diameter of soil grains

γ_w = unit weight of water

η = viscosity of fluid (water)

e = void ratio of the soil

Viscosity and unit weight of water depend upon temperature, hence the coefficient of permeability is effected by the climatic conditions. Constant C depends upon the arrangement and shape of soil grains and voids.

The coefficient of permeability may be determined both in the laboratory and field. In the laboratory, constant head method and variable head methods are available.

APPLICATION

Water flowing through the soil exerts considerable seepage forces, which has direct effect on the safety of hydraulic structures. The quantity of water escaping through and beneath an earthen dam depends on the permeability of the embankment and the foundation soil respectively. The pore water pressure in the earthen embankment reduces the effective stresses in the soil leading to reduction in the shear resistance of soil slopes. High velocity of flow through the structure of embankment or its foundation leads to piping action. The rate of settlement of foundation depends on the permeability properties of the foundation soil. Higher the permeability of soil, higher the rate of settlement. Shear strength of soil also indirectly depends on its permeability; because dissipation of pore water pressure depends upon its permeability. Approximate values of coefficient of permeability for different types of soil are given in Table 10.1

TABLE 10.1

Permeability of different soils

Type of soil	Value of K (cm/sec)
Gravel	10^3-1.0
Sand	10-10^{-3}
Silt	10^{-3}-10^{-6}
Clay	<10^{-6}

According to US Bureau of reclamation, soils are classified as follows:

Impervious	$K < 10^{-6}$ cm/sec
Semi-pervious	10^{-6} cm/sec $< K < 10^{-4}$ cm/sec
Pervious	$K > 10^{-4}$ cm/sec

APPARATUS

1. Permeability mould with accessories
2. Compaction device (if remoulded sample has to be tested)
3. Constant head reservoir
4. Graduated glass stand pipe
5. Supporting frame and clamps
6. Funnel
7. Measuring flask
8. Stop watch

PROCEDURE

(a) Variable head method

1. Compact the soil into the mould at a given dry density and moisture content by a suitable static or dynamic device for remoulded sample. For undisturbed samples, trim of the undisturbed specimen in the form of cylinder. Place the specimen centrally over the bottom porous disc and filter paper. Fill the annular space between the mould and the specimen with an impervious material such as cement slurry or bentonite slurry to provide sealing against leakage from the sides.
2. Place a filter paper, porous stone and washer on top of the soil sample and fix the top collar.
3. Connect the standpipe to the inlet of the top plate. Fill the standpipe with water.
4. Connect the reservoir with water to the outlet at the bottom of the mould and allow the water to flow through and ensure complete saturation of the sample.
5. Open the air valve at the top and allow the water to flow out so that the air in the cylinder is removed.

6. Fix the height h_1 and h_2 on the pipe from the top of water level in the reservoir as shown in Fig. 10.1 ($h_1 - h_2$ may be around 50 cm).

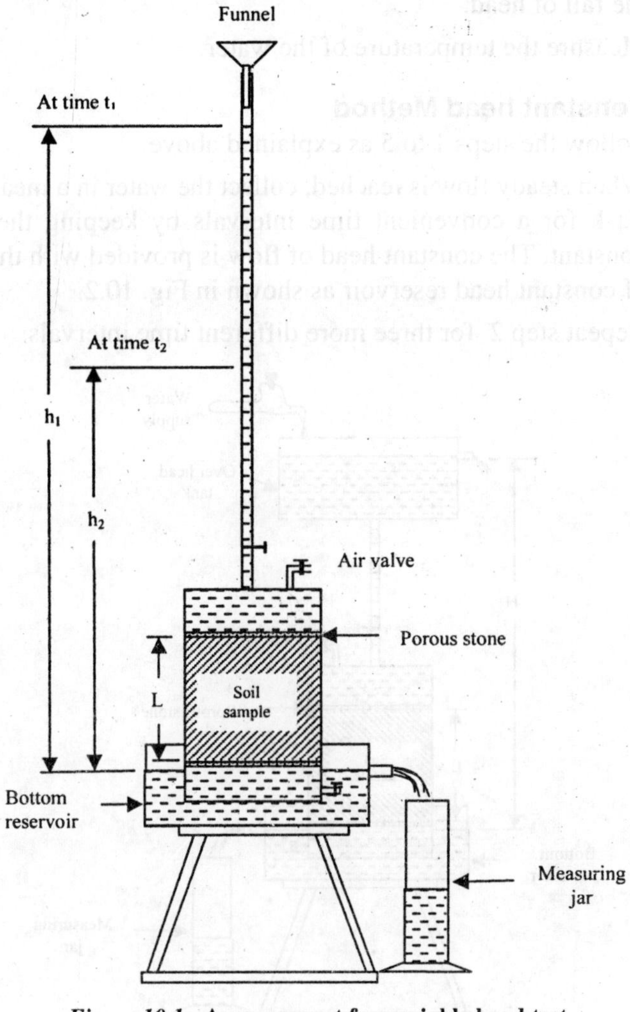

Figure 10.1 **: Arrangement for variable head test**

7. When all the air has escaped, close the air valve and allow the water from the pipe to flow through the soil and establish a steady flow.

8. Record the time required for the water head (in the standpipe) to fall from h_1 to h_2.
9. Change the height h_1 and h_2 and record the time required for the fall of head.
10. Measure the temperature of the water.

(b) Constant head Method

1. Follow the steps 1 to 5 as explained above.
2. When steady flow is reached, collect the water in a measuring flask for a convenient time intervals by keeping the head constant. The constant head of flow is provided with the help of constant head reservoir as shown in Fig. 10.2.
3. Repeat step 2 for three more different time intervals.

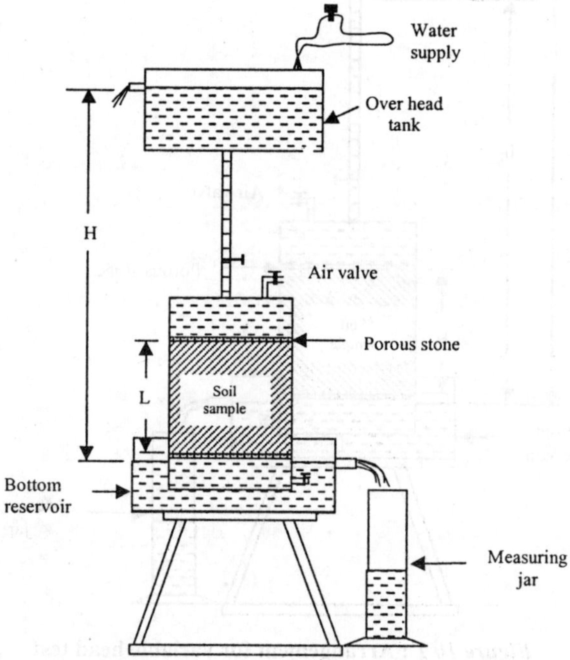

Figure 10.2 **: Arrangement for constant head method**

PRECAUTIONS

1. All the possibilities of leakage at the joints must be eliminated.

All the joints and washer must be thoroughly cleaned so that there are no soil particles between them.

2. Rubber washers must be moistured with water before placing.
3. Porous stones must be saturated before placing.
4. Soil sample must be fully saturated before taking the observations.
5. In order to ensure laminar flow conditions, coarse-grained soil must be tested under low hydraulic gradient.
6. In constant head method, quantity of water collected must be sufficient to and measured accurately to eliminate errors.

Note: The constant head method is more suitable for coarse-grained soils as the quantity of the seepage is more in pervious soils. If the variable head method is employed, the rate of fall of water column in the stand-pipe will be rapid and the recording accurately of the time required for the fall of head from h_1 to h_2 becomes difficult. Similarly, variable head method is suitable for fine-grained soil, as sufficient quantity of water cannot be collected in a small time. If there is any error in measuring the volume of water, the % error will be more (as the total quantity of water collected is less).

OBSERVATIONS AND CALCULATIONS

(*a*) Enter all the observations of variable head method in Table 10.2 and constant head method in Table 10.3.

(*b*) Calculate the coefficient of permeability of soil using the following equations

$$K_T = 2.303\ aL/(At)\ \text{Log10}(h_1/h_2) \quad \text{(Variable head method)}$$

where

K_T = coefficient of permeability at test temperature T°C (cm/sec)

a = cross sectional area of stand pipe (cm^2)

L = effective length of the soil sample (cm)

A = cross sectional area of soil sample (cm^2)

t = time required for the head to fall from h_1 to h_2 (sec)

h_1 = initial head of water in the stand pipe above the water level in the reservoir (cm)

h_2 = final head of water in the stand pipe above the water level in the reservoir (cm)

$K_T = QL/(Aht)$ (constant head method)

where

K_T = coefficient of permeability at test temperature T°C (cm/sec)

Q = quantity of water collected in time t (cc)

L = effective length of the soil sample (cm)

A = cross sectional area of soil sample (cm^2)

h = constant hydraulic head (cm)

(*c*) Report the coefficient of permeability at a given temperature (say at 27°C)

$$K_{27} = K_T \times (\eta_T / \eta_{27})$$

where

K_{27} = coefficient of permeability at 27°C

K_T = coefficient of permeability at T°C

η_T = coefficient of viscosity at T°C

η_{27} = coefficient of viscosity at 27°C

Some typical values of η of water at a few temperatures in milliposes

$\eta_{15} = 11.45$; $\eta_{20} = 10.09$; $\eta_{25} = 8.95$; $\eta_{30} = 8.00$; $\eta_{35} = 7.21$

TABLE 10.2

Observations for variable head method

(*i*) Diameter of stand pipe (cm) =

(*ii*) Cross sectional area of stand pipe, a (cm^2) =

(*iii*) Temperature of water during testing, T (°C) =

(*iv*) Correction factor due to temperature, C_t (= η_T/η_{27}) =

(v) Cross sectional area of the soil sample, A (cm^2) =

(vi) Length of soil sample, L (cm) =

Sl. No.	Initial head h_1 (cm)	Final head h_2 (cm)	Time, t (sec)	K_T (cm/sec)	K_{27} (cm/sec)
1					
2					
3					
4					
5					

TABLE 10.3

Observations for constant head method

(i) Temperature of water during testing, T (°C) =

(ii) Correction factor due to temperature, C_t (= η_T/η_{27}) =

(iii) Cross sectional area of the soil sample, A (cm^2) =

(iv) Length of soil sample, L (cm) =

Sl. No.	Hydraulic head, h (cm)	Time interval t (sec)	Quantity of water collected (cc)	K_T (cm/sec)	K_{27} (cm/sec)
1					
2					
3					
4					
5					

QUESTIONS

1. What is meant by permeability and coefficient of permeability of soil?
2. What is laminar and turbulent flow? What type of flow do you expect in soils?
3. If there are two soils A and B with the following properties, compare their coefficient of permeability:

	Soil A	Soil B
Void ratio	0.4	0.8
Grain size	2mm	1mm

4. What is the effect of temperature of water on coefficient of permeability?
5. How is the value of average coefficient of permeability evaluated in a stratified deposit if the flow were (*i*) parallel and (*ii*) perpendicular to the bedding planes? Which value is greater?
6. What is the unit of coefficient of permeability ? What is the range of its value for gravel, sand, silt and clay?
7. What are the field applications of coefficient of permeability of soils?
8. What is the effect of entrapped air in the voids of soils on the coefficient of permeability? How do you ensure the removal of this air during your experiment?
9. For fine-grained soils which method of permeability test is suitable? Why?
10. How does permeability effects the consolidation of a soil?

11

DETERMINATION OF LIQUID LIMIT AND PLASTIC LIMIT OF SOIL

AIM

(*i*) To determine liquid limit

(*ii*) To determine plastic limit

(*iii*) To classify the soil

(*iv*) To find flow index

(*v*) To find toughness index

THEORY AND APPLICATION

Liquid limit is the water content (expressed in %) at which the soil passes from zero strength to an infinitesimal strength, hence the true value of liquid limit cannot be determined. For determination purpose liquid limit is that water content at which a part of soil, cut by a groove of standard dimensions, will flow together for a distance of 12.5 mm under an impact of 25 blows in a standard liquid limit apparatus with a height of fall of 1 cm.

The moisture content (expressed in %) at which the soil has the smallest plasticity is called the plastic limit. Just after plastic limit the soil displays the properties of a semi-solid.

For determination purposes, the plastic limit is defined as the water content at which a soil just begins to crumble when rolled into a thread of 3 mm in diameter.

The difference in moisture content between the liquid and plastic limits is termed as the plasticity index. Knowing the liquid limit and plasticity index, soil can be classified with the help of plasticity chart (IS: 1498-1970) as shown in Fig. 11.1.

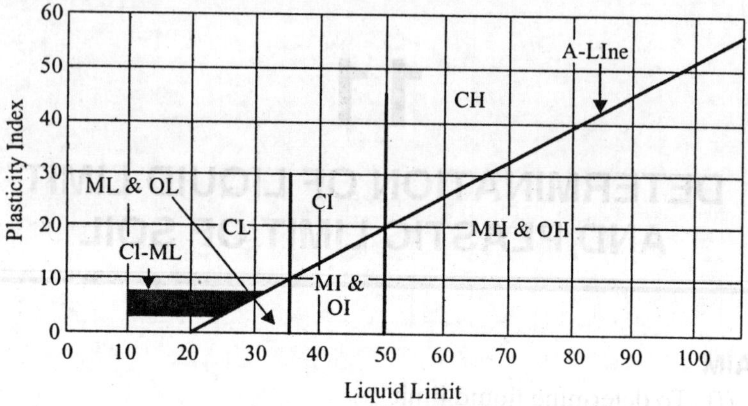

Figure 11.1 **: Plasticity chart**

In the plasticity chart the following symbols are used:

CL = clay of low compressibility

CI = clay of medium (intermediate) compressibility

CH = clay of high compressibility

ML = silt of low compressibility

MI = silt of medium compressibility

MH = silt of high compressibility

OL = organic soil of low compressibility

OI = organic soil of medium compressibility

OH = organic soil of high compressibility

APPLICATIONS

The values of liquid limit and plastic limit are directly used for classifying the fine-grained soils. Once the soil is classified, it helps in understanding the behaviour of soils and selecting the suitable method of design, construction and maintenance of the structures made up or/and resting on soils.

APPARATUS

1. Casagrande liquid limit device.
2. Grooving tool (Casagrande type)
3. Glass plate
4. 425µ sieve
5. 3 mm diameter rod
6. Spatula
7. Water content bins
8. Drying oven
9. Sensitive balance
10. Mixing bowl
11. Wash bottle

PROCEDURE

(a) Liquid limit

1. Adjust the cup of liquid limit apparatus with the help of grooving tool gauge and the adjustment plate to give a drop of exactly 1cm on the point of contact on the base.
2. Take about 120g of an air-dried soil sample passing 425µ sieve.
3. Mix the soil thoroughly with some distilled water to form a uniform paste.
4. Place a portion of the paste in the cup of the liquid limit device; smooth the surface with spatula to a maximum depth of 1cm. Draw the grooving tool through the sample along the symmetrical axis of the cup, holding the tool perpendicular to the cup.
5. Turn the handle at a rate of 2 revolutions per second and count the blows until the two parts of the soil sample come in contact with each other, at the bottom of the groove, along a distance of 10 mm.
6. Transfer about 15g of the soil sample forming the wedge of the grove that flowed together to a water content bin, and determine the water content by oven drying.

7. Transfer the remaining soil in the cup to the main soil sample in the bowl and mix thoroughly after adding a small amount of water.
8. Repeat steps 4 to 7. Obtain at least five sets of readings in the range of 10-40 blows.
9. Record the observations in Table 11.1

(b) Plastic Limit

1. Take about 30g of air-dried soil sample passing through 425µ sieve.
2. Mix thoroughly with distilled water on the glass plate until it is plastic enough to be shaped into a small ball.
3. Take about 10 g of the plastic soil mass and roll it between the hand and the glass plate to form the soil mass into a thread of as small diameter as possible. If the diameter of the thread becomes less than 3 mm without cracks, it indicates that the water added to the soil is more than its plastic limit, hence the soil is kneaded further and rolled into thread again.
4. Repeat this rolling and remoulding process until the thread start just crumbling at a diameter of 3mm.
5. If the soil sample start crumbling before the diameter of thread reaches 3 mm (i.e. when the diameter is more than 3 mm) in step 3, it shows that water added in step 2 is less than the plastic limit of the soil. Hence, some more water should be added and mixed to a uniform mass and rolled again, until the thread starts just crumbling at a diameter of 3 mm.
6. Collect the piece of crumbled soil thread at 3 mm diameter in an airtight container and determine moisture content.
7. Repeat this procedure on the remaining masses of 10 g.
8. Record the observations in Table 11.1 and obtain the average value of plastic limit.

PRECAUTIONS

1. Soil used for liquid limit and plastic limit determinations should not be oven dried prior to testing.
2. In liquid limit test, the groove should be closed by the flow

of soil and not by slippage between the soil and the cup.

3. After mixing the water to the soil sample, sufficient time should be given to permeate the water throughout the soil mass.
4. Wet soil taken in the container for moisture content determination should not be left open in the air, the container with soil sample should either be placed in desiccator or immediately be weighed.

OBSERVATIONS AND CALCULATIONS

(a) Liquid limit (LL)

1. Use Table 11.1 for recording number of blows and calculating the moisture contents.
2. Use semi-log graph paper. Take number of blows on log-scale (X-axis) and water content on normal scale (Y-axis). Plot all the points and draw a straight line (flow curve) passing through these points.
3. Read the water content at 25 blows, which is the value of liquid limit.

TABLE 11.1

Observations for liquid limit

Trial No.		1	2	3	4	5
1. No. blows						
2. Container (bin) No.						
3. Weight of container + wet soil	(g)					
4. Weight of container + dry soil	(g)					
5. Weight of water (3) – (4)	(g)					
6. Weight of container	(g)					
7. Weight of dry soil (4) – (6)	(g)					
8. Moisture content, m (5)/(7)						
9. Moisture content (%) m x 100						
Moisture content corresponding to 25 blows (LL), from graph =						

RESULT

Liquid limit = ____________________

(b) Plastic Limit (PL)

Use the Table 11.2 for calculating the plastic limit of the soil.

TABLE 11.2

Observations for plastic limit

Trial No.		1	2	3	4	5
1. Container (bin) No.						
2. Weight of container + wet soil	(g)					
3. Weight of container + dry soil	(g)					
4. Weight of water (2) – (3)	(g)					
5. Weight of container	(g)					
6. Weight of dry soil (3) – (5)	(g)					
7. Moisture content, m (5)/(7)						
8. Moisture content (%) m x 100 (Plastic limit)						
9. Average value of plastic limit						

RESULT

Average value of Plastic limit =

(c) Classification of Soil

1. Calculate the Plasticity index (PI)

   PI = LL – PL

2. Use plasticity chart for classification of given soil

   Calculate the plasticity of A-line

   $(PI)_A = 0.73\,(LL - 30)$

   where LL is liquid limit

   If PI > $(PI)_A$ the soil is clay

   If PI < $(PI)_A$ the soil is silt

   If LL = 0-35 low compressibility

   If LL = 35-50 medium compressibility and

   If LL > 50 high compressibility

(d) Flow Index (FI)

1. Extend the flow curve at both the ends so as to intersect the ordinates corresponding to 10 and 100 blows.

2. Read the water content at 10 and 100 blows. Difference of these two water contents is called flow index or
   The flow index may be calculated from the equation as

   $$FI = (W_1 - W_2)/\{(\log_{10}(N_2/N_1)\}$$

   Where

   W_1 = water content in % at N_1 blows

   W_2 = water content in % at N_2 blows

(e) Toughness index (TI)

Toughness Index TI = Plasticity index/Flow index = PI/FI

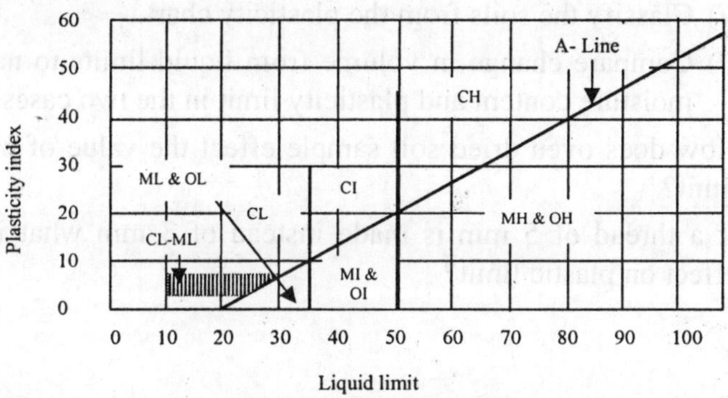

Figure 11.1 : **Plasticity chart**

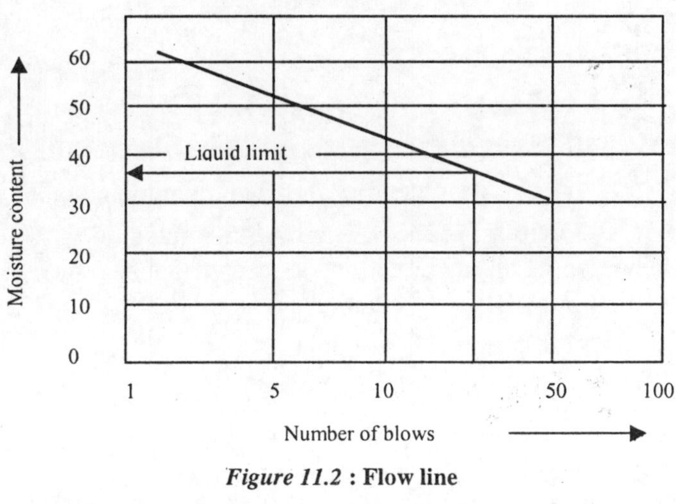

Figure 11.2 : **Flow line**

QUESTIONS

1. How the plastic limit is defined to determine it in the laboratory?
2. What is the degree of saturation at liquid limit and Plastic Limit?
3. There are two soils with the following properties:

Soil	Liquid limit	Plastic limit	Natural Moisture content (%)
A	70	30	40
B	55	25	40

   (*i*) Classify the soils from the plasticity chart.

   (*ii*) Compare change in volume from liquid limits to natural moisture content and plasticity limit in the two cases.

4. How does oven dried soil sample effect the value of plastic limit?
5. If a thread of 5 mm is made instead of 3 mm what is the effect on plastic limit?

12

DETERMINATION OF COEFFICIENT OF CONSOLIDATION

AIM

To determine the coefficient of consolidation of a given clay soil.

THEORY AND APPLICATION

When a load is applied on a saturated soil, the load will initially be transferred to the water in pores of the soil (called pore water). This results in development of pressure in pore water (pore pressure), which results in the escape of water from voids and brings the soil particles together. The process of escape of water under applied load, leads to reduction in volume of voids and hence the volume of soil. The process of reduction of volume of voids due to expulsion of water under sustained static load is known as consolidation. The magnitude of consolidation depends on the amount of voids or void ratio of the soil. The rate of consolidation depends on the permeability properties of soil. The two important consolidation properties of soil are (*i*) coefficient of consolidation (C_v) and (*ii*) compression index (C_c). The coefficient of consolidation reflects the behaviour of soil with respect to time under a given load intensity. Dimensional formula for C_v is L^2T^{-1}. Compression index explains the behaviour of soils under increased loads. It has no units. The testing procedure of compression index is explained in Chapter Thirteen.

APPLICATIONS

Consolidation properties are required in estimating the settlement of a foundation. They provide the maximum amount of settlements under a given load and the time required for it to occur. Many times the design of foundation is carried out based on the limiting settlements. The amount of consolidation will be more in clay soils. Further, due to low permeability, the rate of settlement in clay soil is very low. That means the time required for the total settlement in clay soils is very high. Hence, the study of consolidation properties is important for foundations resting on clay soil.

APPARATUS

1. Consolidometer consisting of specimen ring
2. Guide ring
3. Porous stones
4. Dial gauges
5. Stop watch

Specimen dimensions are 60mm diameter and 20mm thick.

PROCEDURE

Preparation of specimen

Sufficient thickness of the soil specimen is cut from undisturbed sample. The consolidation ring is gradually inserted into the sample by pressing and carefully removing the material around it. The specimen should be trimmed smooth and flush to the ends of the ring. Any voids in the specimen caused due to removal of gravel are lime stone pieces should be filled back by pressing completely the loose soil in the voids. The ring should be wiped clean and weighed again with the soil. Place wet filter paper on top and bottom faces of the sample and two porous stones covering it should be place. Placed this assembly in the loading frame. Over the porous stone a perforated plate with loading ball is placed as shown in Fig. 12.1.

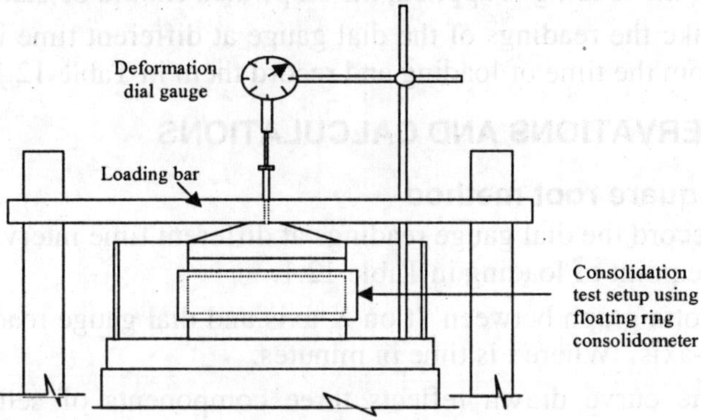

(*a*) Consolidometer

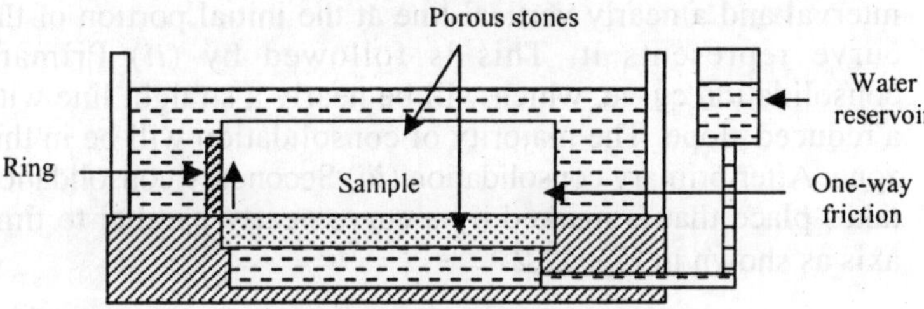

(*b*) Fixed-ring consolidometer

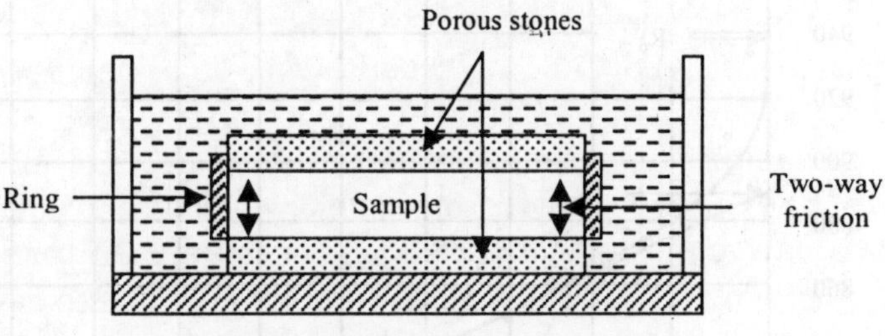

(*c*) Floating-ring consolidometer

Figure 12.1 **: Line diagram of a typical consolidation test apparatus**

The sample is put for saturation both from top and bottom (bottom through a reservoir). After allowing time for saturation, the load is applied through the loading frame. The settlement in sample is measured using a dial gauge. The stepwise procedure for observing reading is as follows:

1. Apply the required load intensity (stress) at which C_v is to be determined.

2. As the loading is applied, the stopwatch should be started.
3. Take the readings of the dial gauge at different time interval from the time of loading and record them in Table 12.1.

OBSERVATIONS AND CALCULATIONS

(a) Square root method

1. Record the dial gauge readings at different time interval from the point of loading in Table 12.1.
2. Plot a graph between √t on X-axis and dial gauge reading on Y-axis. Where t is time in minutes.
3. The curve drawn reflects three components of settlement (*i*) Immediate settlement or elastic compression. This will be reflected in the form of steep settlements in a small time interval and a nearly vertical line at the initial portion of the curve represents it. This is followed by (*ii*) Primary consolidation curve, which will be nearly a straight line with a reduced slope. The majority of consolidation will be in this zone. After primary consolidation (*iii*) Secondary consolidation takes place that is marked by a curve nearly parallel to time axis as shown in Fig. 12.2.

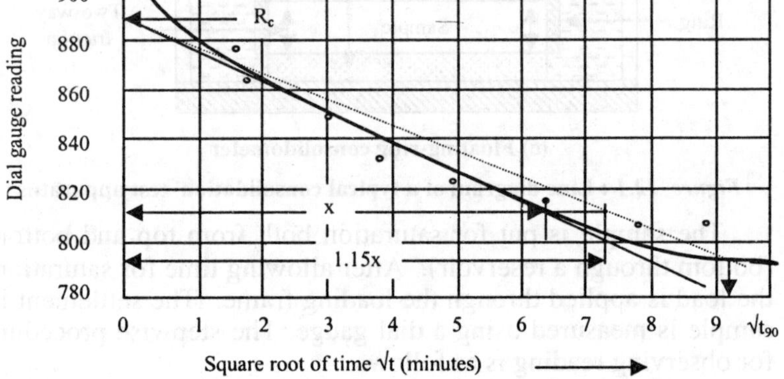

Figure 12.2 : **Square root time versus dial gauge reading**

4. Draw a straight line through a primary consolidation zone (i.e. straight line passing through the points covered in this zone). Identification of primary consolidation zone depends on experience and eye judgement. Extent the straight line to meet Y-axis at O_c. O_c is the corrected zero.
5. Draw another straight line through O_c, with a slope equal to 1.15 times the slope of the earlier straight line.
6. The straight line so drawn (with 1.15 times the slope of primary consolidation line) will intersect the originally plotted curve at a point. The X-coordinate of this point will give $\sqrt{t_{90}}$. Where t_{90} is the time required for 90% consolidation (in minutes).
7. The coefficient of consolidation is calculated as follows

$$C_v = 0.848\ H^2/(\ t_{90} \times 60) \qquad (cm^2/sec)$$

where H = length of drainage path (cm)

(= half the thickness of soil sample for double drainage and = thickness of the sample for single drainage)

t_{90} = time required for 90% consolidation in minutes

(b) Log-method

1. The compression dial readings should be plotted against the log of time and a smooth curve drawn to pass through the points.
2. The two straight portions of the curve should be extended to intersect at a point, the ordinate of which gives d_{100} corresponding to 100% primary compression.
3. The corrected zero point d_s, shall be located by the laying of above point in the neighbourhood of 0.1minute a distance equal to the vertical distance between this point and one at a time which is four times this value (several pairs of points with time ratios of 4 may be used; pairs up to 5 minutes/ 20minutes or 10minutes/40 minutes may be needed for soils of higher plasticity. The corrected zero point may be based on the best value obtained from these pairs of points).

4. The 50% compression point which is halfway between the corrected zero point and the 100% compression point, shall be marked on the curve and the readings on the time axis corresponding to this point t_{50}, time to 50% primary compression, shall be noted. The readings, on the dial gauge reading axis, corresponding to 100% compression gives d_{100}.
5. Coefficient of consolidation is calculated as follows:

$$C_v = 0.197\ H^2/t_{50}$$

QUESTIONS

1. What are the units of coefficient of consolidation?
2. What do you understand by single drainage and double drainage?
3. What do you understand by the term length of drainage path? Explain.
4. What is the use of coefficient of consolidation in field problems?
5. What is the role of permeability of soil on coefficient of consolidation?
6. What do you understand by elastic settlement, primary consolidation and secondary consolidation? Which one among these is important? Explain.
7. Why consolidation tests are done mainly on clay? Why not on sand or gravel?
8. During consolidation tests, why do we keep the sample saturated? If the sample is tested under unsaturated condition what happens? Explain.
9. What is the need of porous stone in consolidation test? If we keep only perforated plate, without porous stone, what happens?

TABLE 12.1

Coefficient of consolidation

Dimensions of sample: Diameter = Thickness =

Unit weight of soil =

Elapsed time in minutes, t	√t	Dial gauge reading
(1)	(2)	(3)
0	0	
0.25	0.50	
2.25	1.50	
4.00	2.00	
6.25	2.50	
9.00	3.00	
12.25	3.50	
16.00	4.00	
20.25	4.50	
25.00	5.00	
36.00	6.00	
49.00	7.00	
64.00	8.00	
81.00	9.00	
100.00	10.00	
121.00	11.00	
144.00	12.00	
169.00	13.00	
196.00	14.00	
225.00	15.00	
256.00	16.00	

13

DETERMINATION OF COMPRESSION INDEX OF SOIL

AIM

To determine the compression index of the given soil.

THEORY AND APPLICATION

Consolidation is the process of reduction of void space due to expulsion of water from pores under constantly applied static load. The consolidation properties of soil required to estimate settlement behaviour of foundation. The two aspects of foundation settlement are (*i*) rate of settlement and (*ii*) total settlement under a given load. The rate of settlement is estimated using coefficient of consolidation, discussed in Chapter Twelve. The amount of total settlement is estimated using compression index, which is discussed in this chapter.

APPARATUS

1. Loading Device: a suitable device for application of loads to the soil specimen. The loading may be applied either by a jack with load measurement arrangement or by the lever system on which weights of known magnitude can be hung. The lever system shall be such that no horizontal force is imposed on the specimen at any stage during testing and should ensure verticality of all loads applied to the specimen.
2. Consolidometer: a device to hold the sample in a ring either fixed or floating with porous stones on each face of the sample

(Fig. 12.1). A consolidometer shall also provide means for submerging the sample, for applying a vertical load and for measuring the change in the thickness of the specimen. Suitable provision shall be made to enable the dial gauge to be fixed in such a way that the dial gauge records accurately the vertical compression of the specimen. The consolidometer shall allow compression of specimen to 50% of its original thickness.

3. Porous stones: The porous stones shall be of silicon carbide, aluminium oxide or porous metal and medium grade. It shall have a high permeability compared to that of the soil being tested.
4. Soil trimming tools: like fine wire-saw, knife, spatula, etc, for trimming sample to fit into the inside diameter of the consolidometer ring with a minimum of disturbance.
5. Water reservoir to saturate the soil sample.
6. Balance with sensitivity of 0.01 g.
7. Dial gauge with a least count of 0.002 mm.
8. Oven to maintain the temperature between 105° and 110°C.
9. Dessicator with any desiccating agent other than Sulphuric acid.
10. Moisture content bins.

PROCEDURE

(A) Preparation of the Soil Specimen

(*i*) **Preparation of specimen from undisturbed soil sample:** The container shall be cleaned and weighed empty. About 3 cm or more if desired from one end of the undisturbed soil sample shall be cut off and rejected. The specimen shall be cut off either from the undisturbed tube samples or from block sample, the latter generally being more representative of the field conditions. In either case the consolidation ring should be gradually inserted in the sample by pressing with hands and carefully removing the material around the ring. The soil specimen so cut shall project as far as 1 cm on either side of the ring. The specimen shall then be trimmed smooth and flush with the top and bottom of the ring. Any voids in the specimen caused due to removal of gravel or limestone pieces, shall be filled back by pressing lightly the loose soil in the voids, care being taken to see that the permeability of the specimen is not affected. The container ring shall be weighed again with soil. Three representative specimens from the soil trimmings shall be taken to determine the moisture content.

(*ii*) **Preparation of specimen from representative soil sample:** In cases where it is necessary to use disturbed soil samples, the soil sample shall be compacted to the desired (or field) density at the desired (or field) water content in a larger container (say Proctor mould) and the required specimen for the test prepared as explained above from the compacted sample.

ASSEMBLY

The porous stones shall be saturated, by boiling them in distilled water for at least 15minutes. All surfaces of the consolidometer, which are to be enclosed, shall be moistened. The consolidometer shall be assembled with the soil specimen (in the ring) and porous stones at top and bottom of the specimen, providing a filter paper between the soil specimen and the porous stone. The loading block shall then be positioned centrally on the top porous stone.

This assembly shall be mounted on the loading frame such that, the load when applied is transmitted to the soil specimen through the loading cap.

The holder with the dial gauge to record the progressive vertical compression of the specimen under load, shall than be screwed in place and adjusted in such a way that the dial gauge is near the beginning of its release run, allowing sufficient swelling of the soil if any.

The system shall be connected to a water reservoir with the level of water in the reservoir being at about the same level as the soil specimen and water allowed to flow in the sample. The soil shall be allowed to saturate.

LOADING

1. The compression dial reading, about 24 hours after the application of the initial seating load (about 0.05 kg/cm^2), shall be noted.
2. Apply a normal load to give the desired pressure intensity on soil (initially say 0.25 kg/cm^2).
3. Record the dial gauge readings with time till it undergoes 90% of primary consolidation for slow consolidating soils, the consolidation may extend up to about 24 hours. Take the final reading of settlement dial gauge reading under the applied load intensity after 24 hours.
4. After taking the reading, the load intensity on the soil is doubled. The dial gauge readings with time shall be observed as explained earlier and the final reading after 24 hours of applied load be taken as the final reading for the increased load.
5. The above steps are repeated by doubling the load intensity every time and noting the corresponding final dial gauge readings.
6. After the last load (about 16kg/cm^2) has been on, for the required period, the load should be decreased to one-fourth the value of the last load and allowed to stand for 24 hours. The load shall be further reduced in steps of one-fourth the previous intensity till an intensity of 0.1 kg/cm^2 is reached. If data for repeated loading is desired, the load intensity may now be increased in steps of double the immediately preceding value and the observations repeated.
7. When the observations mentioned above are completed, the soil specimen assembly be dismantled, the excess surface water on the soil specimen carefully removed by blotting, and the ring with the consolidated soil specimen weighed. The soil shall then be dried to constant weight in an oven maintaining at 105° to 110°C and the dry weight recorded.

OBSERVATIONS AND CALCULATIONS

Record the observations in the Tables 13.1 and 13.2

The equivalent height of the soil solids shall be calculated as follows:

$$2H_o = W_s/(G_s\gamma_w A)$$

where

$2H_o$ = equivalent thickness of solids

W_s = weight of soil solids as determined by oven drying the specimen at the end of the test

G_s = specific gravity of soil solids

γ_w = unit weight of water

A = area of container ring

From the initial thickness of the soil sample and the final dial gauge readings, the thickness 2H of the sample at the end of each application of load shall be calculated. The void ratio in each case shall be calculated as follows:

$$e = (2H)/(2H_o) - 1$$

where

e = void ratio

$2H$ = thickness of specimen at the end of a specified period after application of each load

$2H_o$ = equivalent thickness of solids

From the calculated void ratios, a plot of void ratio e, versus log of pressure intensity p, is plotted. The initial compression curve would be found to be a straight line at pressures above a certain value. The slope of this straight-line portion of the curve shall be reported as the compression index C_c, which is mathematically given as

$$C_c = (e_o - e)/\log_{10}(p/p_o)$$

where

C_c = compression index

e_o = initial void ratio

e = void ratio under a pressure intensity p

p_o = initial pressure intensity

OBSERVATIONS FOR COMPRESSION INDEX

Project

Measurement of container ring : Weight of container:

Diameter (internal) of container : Area of container

Initial thickness of soil sample, $2H_i$: Specific gravity of soil solids, G_s:

Equivalent height of solids,

$2H_o = W_s/(G_s\gamma_w A)$: Least count of dial gauge :

TABLE 13.1

Observations of test for compression index

Applied Pressure (kg/cm^2) p	Final Dial reading	Change in Dial reading c_{dr}	Change in thickness $c_t = c_{dr} \times LC$ (mm)	Thickness of the soil sample $2H = 2H_i - c_t$ (mm)	Void Ratio $e = 2H/(2H_o) - 1$	C_c

TABLE 13.2

Observations for determination of moisture content (for Consolidation Test)

	Before test	After test
1. Wt. of container ring + wet soil, (w_1)		
2. Wt. of container ring + dry soil, (w_2)		
3. Wt. of ring, (w_3)		
4. Wt. of dry soil, (2) – (3)		
5. Wt. of water, (1) – (2)		
Moisture content, m = (5)/(4)		

RESULTS

Compression Index of the soil =

QUESTIONS

1. What are the units of compression index?
2. Is there any effect of permeability of the value of compression index? If so how does it effect?
3. What happens to the results of compression index, if the soil is not saturated completely during testing?
4. What are the factors that effect the compression index of a soil?

14

DETERMINATION OF UNCONFINED COMPRESSIVE STRENGTH OF THE SOIL

AIM

1. To determine the unconfined compressive strength of the soil.
2. To determine sensitivity of the soil sample.

THEORY AND APPLICATION

The unconfined compressive strength is defined as the ratio of axial failure load to cross sectional area of the soil sample when it is not subjected to any lateral pressure.

$$q_u = P/A_c$$

where

q_u = unconfined compressive strength

P = axial load at failure

A_c = corrected area at failure = $A_o/(1 - \varepsilon)$

A_o = initial cross sectional area

ε = axial strain in the sample $\Delta L/L_o$

ΔL = change in length of the sample

L_o = initial length of the sample

This test is considered as undrained, as the rate of loading does not allow dissipation of pore water pressure.

Sensitivity is defined as the ratio of unconfined compressive strength of undisturbed soil sample to the unconfined compressive strength of remoulded sample at constant moisture content.

$$\text{Sensitivity} = (q_{uu}) / (q_{ur})$$

where

q_{uu} = unconfined compressive strength of undisturbed soil sample

q_{ur} = unconfined compressive strength of remoulded soil sample

Cohesion of the soil sample may be calculated by using the following relations:

$$\sigma_1 = \sigma_3 \text{Tan}^2\alpha + 2C \text{ Tan } \alpha$$

where

σ_1 = major principal stress at failure

σ_3 = minor principal stress at failure

α = failure angle with the major principal plane

= $(45° + \phi/2)$ (ϕ = angle of internal friction of the soil)

In unconfined compression test $\sigma_3 = 0$; $\sigma_1 = q_u$

Hence

$$q_u = 2C \text{ Tan } (45° + \phi/2)$$

$$C = q_u / \{2 \text{ Tan } (45° + \phi/2)\}$$

If the soil is pure cohesive soil, $\phi = 0$, therefore

$$C = q_u / 2$$

APPLICATIONS

This is the simplest and quickest test for determining the cohesion and the shear strength of the cohesive soils. These values are used for checking the short-term stability of foundations and slopes, soil consistency can be known from the value of unconfined compressive strength as shown in Table 14.1.

TABLE 14.1

VARIATION OF CONSISTENCY OF SOIL WITH q_U

q_u (kg/cm^2)	Soil consistency
< 0.25	Very soft
0.25-0.50	Soft
0.50-1.00	Medium
1.00-2.00	Stiff
2.00-4.00	Very stiff
> 4.00	Hard

Sensitivity is a very useful factor to know the effect of remoulding on the shear strength of the cohesive soils. Remoulding of soil is very common during pile driving and excavations. Generally soils having sensitivity less than four are considered good for the construction purposes. Soils are designated as follows with respect to sensitivity.

TABLE 14.2

Sensitivity of soils

Sensitivity	Designation
1 - 4	Normal
4 -8	Sensitive
8 - 15	Extra sensitive
> 15	Quick

There are two methods available to determine the unconfined compressive strength of soil.

1. Screw jack with spring compression as load measuring device.
2. Compression machine with proving ring as load measuring device.

(a) Screw jack method

APPARATUS

1. Unconfined compression apparatus (screw jack with spring load measuring device)

2. Sampling tube of internal diameter 38 mm and 200 mm long.
3. Sample extractor
4. Split mould, internal diameter 38 mm and 76 mm long.
5. Vernier calipers

PROCEDURE

1. Collect the soil sample by pushing the sampling tube into the soil and saturate it by a suitable method if possible.
2. Coat the inside of the split mould with a thin layer of grease or oil.
3. Extrude the specimen from the sampling tube to the split mould with the help of the sample extractor and knife.
4. Determine the density of the specimen.
5. Remove the sample from the split mould and measure its length and diameter.
6. Place the specimen in the compression apparatus.
7. Fix the graph paper and pencil.
8. Apply compressive load by giving about half a turn of the handle per second till the sample failed or 20% strain occurs.
9. Measure the angle of failure plane from the horizontal.
10. Determine the moisture content of the soil sample.

PRECAUTIONS

1. Two ends of the specimen should be perpendicular to the axis of the specimen.
2. The pencil should be fixed carefully so as to press the paper and draw smooth curve.
3. The loading of the sample should be at constant rate.
4. Remoulded specimen should be prepared at the same moisture content and density as of undisturbed sample.

OBSERVATIONS AND CALCULATIONS

1. Note the point of maximum spring extension on the graph paper. Select any three points on the right hand side one point on the left-hand side of the point of the maximum extension.

2. Read the spring extension and deformation corresponding of these points.
3. Calculate the compressive stresses for these points. Maximum stress will give the unconfined compressive strength.
4. If the sample does not fail, stress corresponding to 20% strain is taken as the unconfined compressive strength.
5. Calculate the sensitivity of the soil.

   Sensitivity $= (q_{uu})/(q_{ur})$
6. Calculate the angle of internal friction ϕu, if the failure angle α has been measured for partially saturated samples.

   $\phi_u = 2(\alpha - 45)$
7. Calculate the values of cohesion C_u

   $C_u = q_u/2$ if the sample is fully saturated

   $C_u = q_u/(2 \text{ Tan } \alpha)$ if the sample is partially saturated.

Compression Machine with Proving Ring:

APPARATUS

1. Loading frame
2. Proving ring
3. A dial gauge (0.01 mm least count)

   And other equipment as listed in the screw jack method.

PROCEDURE

1. Prepare the soil sample as explained in screw jack method.
2. Arrange the sample between the moving base and the top plate connected to the proving ring as shown in Fig. 14.1.
3. Rise the platform up, so that the soil sample is subjected to compressive force.
4. Take the dial gauge reading and proving ring readings and record in Table 14.3.
5. The dial gauge reading provides the deformation in the sample and in-turn the strain.
6. The provingring reading provides the corresponding load in-turn the axial stress on the sample.

7. Plot graph between axial stress and axial strain. Obtain the peak stress from the graph (Fig. 14.2). This stress is the unconfined compressive strength of the soil.
   Using the same procedure, the test can be performed using the convention triaxial test apparatus without using confining pressure.

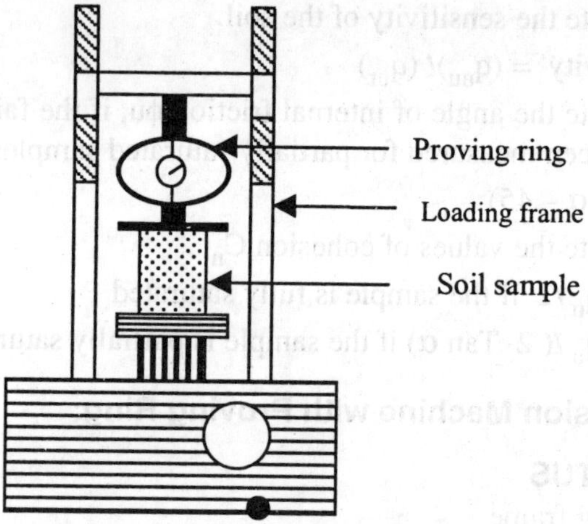

Figure 14.1 **: Unconfined compression test apparatus proving ring type**

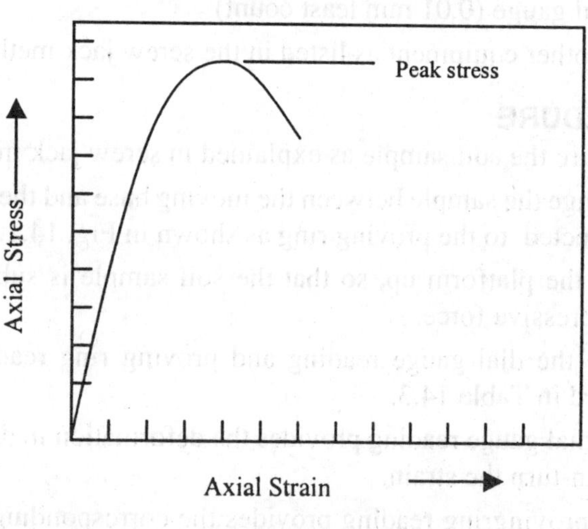

Figure 14.2 **: Axial stress strain graph from unconfined compression test**

TABLE 14.3

Observations for unconfined compression test (proving ring method)

Project name & location of site:

Project report No:

Location of sample:

Sample collected on: Sample collected by:

Sample tested by: Sample tested on:

Density of sample: Moisture content of sample:

Initial length of Sample L_o: Initial cross section of the sample A_o:

Dial gauge	Deformation ΔL (mm)	Strain, ε $= \Delta L/L_o$	Corrected area, A_c $= A_o/(1 - \varepsilon)$	Proving ring Reading	Load, P (Kg)	Stress, σ $= P/A_c$

QUESTIONS

1. What do you understand by unconfined compressive strength of soil?
2. Can you determine unconfined compressive strength for all types of soils? Explain?
3. What is corrected area? How is it obtained?
4. What are the drainage conditions in unconfined compression test?
5. What is the difference between the unconfined compression test and the unconsolidated undrained triaxial test?
6. How do you obtain shear parameters from unconfined compression test?

7. If there are two samples from the same cohesive soil, one wet and the other is fully saturated, what difference do you expect in shear parameters and angle of failure plane?
8. What do you understand by sensitivity? How do you estimate?
9. What do you understand by undisturbed and remoulded soil sample? What are the different field problems, which will govern the selection of type of soil sample for laboratory testing?
10. What is meant by stress controlled and strain controlled tests? Comment on the test conditions explained in this chapter.

15

DETERMINATION OF SHEAR STRENGTH OF SOIL BY VANE SHEAR TEST

AIM

To determine shear strength of clay soil using laboratory vane shear apparatus.

THEORY

In soil, shear strength is contributed by the two properties. (1) Cohesion and (2) Angle of internal friction. In pure clays the shear resistance due to internal friction is negligible. Hence, the complete shear strength in clays, is due to cohesion, (C).

APPARATUS

The vane shear test apparatus consists of a torque head mounted on a bracket. Four shear vanes are fixed on a shaft and the shaft is fixed in the lower end of a circular disk graduated in degrees. A torsion spring is fixed between torque head and the circular disk. A maximum pointer is provided to facilitate reading the angle of torque. As the strain indicating pointer rotates when the torque is applied, it moves the maximum pointer, leaving it in position when the torque get released at failure and the vane returns to its initial position. Turning the torque applicator handle effects rotation of the vane.

PROCEDURE

1. Clean the apparatus thoroughly. Apply grease to the lead screw.
2. Fill-up the sampling mould with remoulded soil at required density and moisture content or the undisturbed soil sample. Level the surface of the sample with the mould.
3. Mount the sampling tube with sample under the base of the unit and clamp it in position.
4. Bring the maximum pointer into contact with the strain-indicating pointer. Note down the initial reading of these pointers on the circular graduated scale.
5. Lower the bracket until the shear vanes go into the soil sample to their full length.
6. Operate the torque applicator handle until the specimen fails, which is indicated by the return of the strain-indicating pointer or rotation of drum.
7. Note down the readings of the maximum pointer.
8. The difference between the two readings (initial and final) gives the angle of torque.
9. Repeat steps 3 to 8, on a number of samples to obtain the average shear strength of the sample.

OBSERVATIONS AND CALCULATIONS

1. Tabulate the observations in Table 15.1.
2. Calculate torque $T = \theta \times K/180$

where

θ = difference of angle (angle of torque)

K = spring factor

3. Shear strength of the soil, C is computed using the following formula

$$T = C\pi\,(d^2h/2 + d^3/6)$$

where

d = diameter of vane (cm)

h = height of the vane (cm)

C = shear strength (kg/cm^2)

T = torque applied (kg-cm)

TABLE 15.1
VANE SHEAR TEST

Project name & location of site:

Project report No:

Location of sample:

Sample collected on: Sample collected by:

Sample tested by: Sample tested on:

Diameter of vane, d, = ; height of vane, h, = ;

spring constant, K =

Sl. No.	Initial Reading, θ_1^o	Final Reading, θ_2^o	Angle of Torque, θ $= \theta_2 - \theta_1$	Torque, T $\theta \times K/180$	Shear strength, C (Kg/cm^2)
Average shear strength of soil, C					

RESULT

Average shear strength of the soil =

QUESTIONS

1. For which type of soil the vane shear test is used?
2. In vane shear test, we obtain the shear strength of the soil but denote it as cohesion, Why?
3. Why do we rotate vanes in clockwise direction only?
4. When soil fails, the spring pointer tries to come back to initial reading but it will not reach the initial reading until we remove the soil sample from the apparatus. Why?
5. How does moisture content effect the shear strength of the soil?

16

DETERMINATION OF SHEAR PARAMETERS OF SOIL BY DIRECT SHEAR TEST

AIM

To determine shear strength parameters of the given soil sample at known density by conducting direct shear test.

THEORY AND APPLICATION

Shear strength of a soil is its maximum resistance to shearing stresses. It is equal to the shear stress at failure on the failure plane. Shear strength is composed of : (*i*) internal frictions, which is the resistance due to the friction between the individual particles at their contact points and inter locking of particles. (*ii*) cohesion which is the resistance due to inter-particle forces, which tend to hold the particles together in a soil mass. Coulomb has represented the shear strength of the soils by the equation:

$$\tau_f = C + \sigma \text{Tan } \phi$$

where

τ_f = shear strength of the soil (shear stress at failure)

C = cohesion

σ = normal stress on the failure plane

ϕ = angle of internal friction

The parameters C and ϕ are not constant for a type of soil but it depend on its degree of saturation and the condition of the laboratory testing. In direct shear test, initially a normal stress is applied on the soil specimen. Under the normal stress the pore water pressure gets dissipated leading to the consolidation of the soil under the normal stress is known as consolidation stage. After the application of normal stress, shear stress is applied. During the application of shear stress there will be development of a pore pressure or suction pressure (in very stiff clays and in very dense sands suction pressures develop during shear). If the shear stress is applied at a very slow rate the developed pore pressure gets dissipated. This process of applying shear stress is known as stage of shearing. Depending on whether the dissipation of pore pressure is allowed or not during the application of consolidation and shear load, the shear tests are classified as follows.

(*a*) **Undrained test:** In this, water is not allowed to drain out during the entire test (i.e. during consolidation and shearing), hence there is no dissipation of pore pressures.

(*b*) **Consolidated undrained test:** In this, the soil is allowed to consolidate under the initially applied normal stress only, hence drainage is permitted under normal stress. But no drainage is allowed during shear.

(*c*) **Drained test:** In this, the drainage is allowed throughout the test during the application of both normal and shear stresses. No pore water pressure is setup at any stage of the test.

APPLICATION

Shear parameters are used in the design of earthen dams and embankments. The stability of the failure wedges depends on the shear resistance of the soil along the failure plane. These strength parameters C and ϕ are used in calculating the bearing capacity of soil-foundation systems. The bearing capacity of foundations are estimated using Terzaghi's bearing capacity equation or any other bearing capacity equation. For example the ultimate net bearing capacity of a strip footing is given by the following equation

$$Q_u = CN_c + (N_q - 1)\,\gamma D_f + 0.5\,\gamma BN_\gamma$$

where

Q_u = ultimate bearing capacity of foundation

C = cohesion of foundation soil

D_f = depth of foundation

B = width of footing

γ = unit weight of soil

N_c, N_q & N_γ = bearing capacity factors (functions of ϕ)

Further, shear parameters help in estimating the earth pressures behind the retaining the walls. The values of these parameters are also used in checking the stability of normal slopes, cuts and fills.

APPARATUS

1. Shear box (size 60mm x 60mm x 50mm)
2. Container for shear box
3. Grid plates
4. Base plate
5. Porous stones
6. Loading pad
7. Loading frame
8. Proving ring with dial gauge
9. Static/dynamic compaction device
10. Dial gauge
11. Sample trimmer
12. Balance
13. Oven

PROCEDURE

1. Prepare a soil specimen of size 60 mm × 60 mm × 20 mm, either from an undisturbed soil sample or from a remoulded sample. Soil specimen may also be directly prepared in the box by compaction.
2. Obtain the density of soil specimen.
3. Fix the upper portion of the box to the lower part by fixing pins. Attach the base plate to the lower part.
4. Place the porous stone in the box.

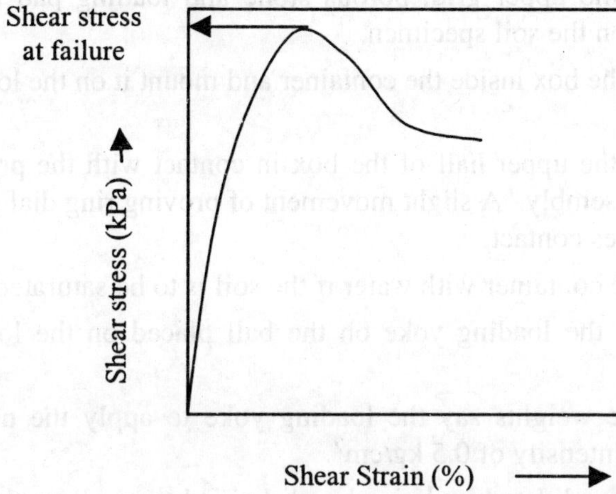

Figure 16.1 **: Shear stress–strain curve**

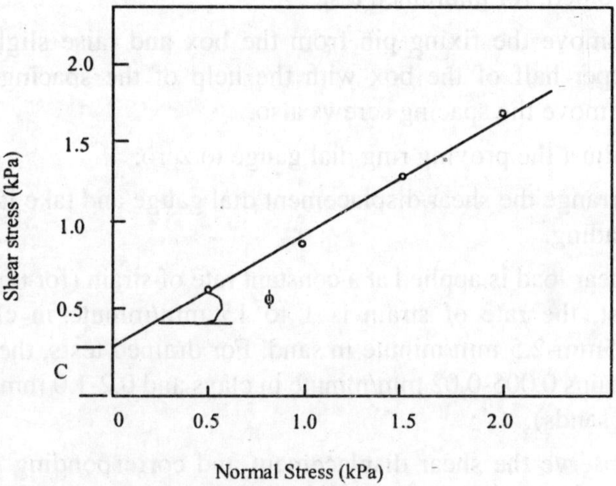

Figure 16.2 **: Failure envelop**

5. For undrained test, place the grid over the porous stone keeping the serrations of the grid at right angle to the direction of the shear. For consolidated undrained and drained tests use the perforated grid in place of plane grid.
6. Transfer the soil specimen prepared in step 1, in the box.

7. Place the upper grid, porous stone and loading pad in the order on the soil specimen.
8. Place the box inside the container and mount it on the loading frame.
9. Bring the upper half of the box in contact with the proving ring assembly. A slight movement of proving ring dial gauge observes contact.
10. Fill the container with water if the soil is to be saturated.
11. Mount the loading yoke on the ball placed on the loading pad.
12. Put the weights say the loading yoke to apply the normal stress intensity of 0.5 kg/cm^2.
13. For consolidated undrained and drained tests allow the soil to consolidate fully under this normal load. This step is avoided, for undrained test.
14. Remove the fixing pin from the box and raise slightly the upper half of the box with the help of the spacing screw. Remove the spacing screws also.
15. Adjust the proving ring dial gauge to zero.
16. Arrange the shear displacement dial gauge and take its initial reading.
17. Shear load is applied at a constant rate of strain (for undrained test, the rate of strain is 1 to 15 mm/minute in clay and 1.5mm-2.5 mm/minute in sand. For drained tests, the rate of strains 0.005-0.02 mm/minute in clays and 0.2-1.0 mm/minute in sands).
18. Observe the shear displacement and corresponding proving ring dial gauge readings. Record the observations in Table 16.1.
19. The reading will increase till the soil fails. Record the proving ring dial gauge reading till the residual stress is reached after failure. (The failure is assumed, when the proving ring dial gauge begins to recede after reaching a maximum or at a shear displacement of approximately 20% of the specimen length.)

20. Plot the graph between the shear stress and shear strain.
21. Repeat the test on identical specimen under increasing normal stress 1, 1.5 and 2 kg/cm^2.

PRECAUTIONS

1. Before starting the test, the upper half of the box should be brought in contact of the proving ring assembly.
2. Before subjecting the specimen to shear, the fixing pins should be taken out.
3. The rate of strain should be constant throughout the test.
4. For drained test, the porous stone should be de-aired and saturated by boiling.

OBSERVATIONS AND CALCULATIONS

1. Obtain the shear force at failure under each normal load, from the graph plotted between the shear stress and shear strain.
2. Record the normal stress and the corresponding shear stress at failure.
3. Plot a graph using normal stress on X-axis and corresponding shear stress at failure on Y-axis. Join the points by a straight line. This is defined as the shear strength envelop.
4. Read the slope of the line, which is defined as the angle of shearing resistance (ϕ) and the intercept of the line with Y-axis, the cohesion of the soil (C).

DIRECT SHEAR TEST OBSERVATIONS

Project name & location of site:

Project report No:

Location of sample:

Sample collected on:

Sample collected by:

Sample tested by:

Sample tested on:

Proving ring constant:

Cross sectional area of the sample (cm^2) =

Thickness of the sample (cm) =

Volume of the sample =

Density of sample=

TABLE 16.1

Observations of shear stress and shear strain

Proving ring constant (k) = ;

Least count or deformation dial gauge =

Normal stress =

Shear deformation dial gauge reading	Proving ring reading	Shear deformation (mm)	Shear strain (%)	Shear load (Proving ring reading × k) (kg)	Shear stress (kg/cm^2)

Normal stress =

Shear deformation dial gauge reading	Proving ring reading	Shear deformation (mm)	Shear strain (%)	Shear load (Proving ring reading × k) (kg)	Shear stress (kg/cm^2)

Normal stress =

Shear deformation dial gauge	Proving ring reading	Shear deformation (mm)	Shear strain (%)	Shear load (Proving ring reading × k) (kg)	Shear stress (kg/cm^2)

Normal stress =

Shear deformation dial gauge	Proving ring reading	Shear deformation (mm)	Shear strain (%)	Shear load (Proving ring reading × k) (kg)	Shear stress (kg/cm^2)

TABLE 16.2

Observations of normal stress and shear stress at failure

Normal stress, σ (kg/cm^2)	Shear stress at failure, τ_f (kg/cm^2)

QUESTIONS

1. What is shear strength of soils? Explain
2. What are shear strength parameters? Are these constant or variable for a given soil?
3. What are undrained, consolidated undrained and drained test? When are they performed?
4. What is the role of pore water pressure on the shear strength of soils?
5. What are the methods to increase the shear strength of soils?
6. What are the other laboratory and field methods to determine shear strength of soils?
7. What are the applications of shear strength parameters in the field problems?
8. Why do you put the grids keeping the serrations at right angles to the direction of shear?
9. Why do you provide space between the two parts of the shear box? How much is it provided?
10. Are you using stress controlled or strain controlled device for direct shear test?
11. What is the rate of strain of your test?

17

DETERMINATION OF SHEAR PARAMETERS OF SOIL BY TRIAXIAL SHEAR TEST

AIM

To determine shear strength parameters of the given soil sample by conducting triaxial shear test.

THEORY AND APPLICATION

Triaxial testing is another test used to measure the shear parameters of a given soil. The test is performed on a cylindrical soil/rock samples. This test is considered to be the most conveniently available test which accommodate a good number of drainage conditions to suit the field situations.

APPARATUS REQUIRED

1. Triaxial testing machine complete with triaxial cell
2. Water pressure unit with hand pump
3. Proving ring
4. Dial gauge
5. Rubber membranes
6. Membrane stretcher
7. Sample trimming apparatus
8. Bins for moisture content determinations.
9. Balance and box of weights
10. Drying oven

PROCEDURE

1. Trim the soil specimen (prepared from the sampling tube of an undisturbed sample tube using universal extractor frame or from a compacted soil specimen as per standard proctor's method, at optimum moisture content or any other moisture content to suite the field situations).Using the trimming apparatus if necessary the trimmed specimen should be 76.2mm long and 38.1mm in diameter. The diameter and the length are measured at not less than 3 places and the average values are used for computations. Note the weight of the specimen (W_1).
2. The specimen is then enclosed in a 38.1mm diameter and about 100mm long rubber membrane, using the membrane stretcher. Spreading back the ends of the membrane over the ends of the stretcher and applying suction between the stretcher and the rubber membranes does this by inhalation. The membrane and the stretcher are then easily slide over the specimen, the suction is released and the membrane is unrolled from the ends of the stretcher.
3. Use non-porous stones on either side of the specimen as neither any pressure is to be measured nor any drainage of air or water is allowed.
4. Remove the porous cylinder from its base removing the bottom fly nuts.
5. The pedestal at the centre of the base of the cylinder on which the specimen is to be placed is cleaned and a 38.1mm diameter rubber O-ring is rolled over to its bottom. The specimen along with the non-porous plate on either side is centrally placed over the pedestal and the bottom edge of the machine covering the specimen is sealed against the pedestal by rolling back the O-ring over the membrane.
6. The cap is placed over the top plate of the specimen and the top of the rubber membrane is sealed against the cap by carefully rolling over it another O-ring. This arrangement of rubber O-ring forms the effective seal between the specimen with the membrane and the water under pressure.The

specimen is checked for its verticality and co-axiality with the cylinder chamber.

7. The chamber (cylinder) along with the loading plunger is carefully placed over its base without disturbing the soil specimen and taking care to see that the plunger rests on the cap of the specimen centrally. The loading frame is then adjusted so that it just touches the plunger top by naked eye. The chamber is then rotated if necessary such that the dial gauge recording compression, rests centrally over the top of the screw which can be locked at any level and which is attached to the top of the cylinder chamber carrying the specimen. The cylinder is then attached to the base plate tightly by means of tightening the nuts.
8. The valve to drain out the chamber and the valve to drain out the air and water from the sample are closed and the air lock nut at the top of the cylinder is kept open to facilitate the exit of air as water enters the chamber through another valve which connects the chamber to the water storage cylinder subjected to a pressure by a hand pump.
9. The water storage cylinder is filled with water completely and its top is then closed by means of a valve. Necessary pressure is built up in the cylinder by working the hand pump and the pressure communicated to the cylinder where the specimen is placed, by opening the connecting valve. The cylindrical chamber is allowed to be filled up completely which is indicated by the emergence of water through the airlock nut at the top of the chamber. Then the airlock nut is closed to develop necessary confining pressure by using the hand pump and the same is maintained constant.
10. If necessary, bring the loading plunger down until it is in contact with the specimen top cap by means of hand operated loading device. This is indicated by a spurt in the reading of the proving ring dial gauge.
11. For this position, adjust the deformation dial gauge reading to zero.

12. Record the initial readings of the proving ring and compression dial gauge.
13. The vertical load is applied to the specimen by starting the motor at the loading frame. The change in the proving ring dial gauge gives the measure of the applied load. The deformation dial gauge gives the deformation in the soil specimen, which can be used to compute strain in the soil.
14. Take the readings of proving ring dial gauge at 0.5, 1.0, 1.5, 2.0% (or any other smaller values) of strain and for every 1.0% strain thereafter up to failure or 20% strain whichever is earlier.
15. Throughout the test, make sure that the chamber, containing pressure is kept constant at the desirable value as indicated by the pressure gauge on the water cylinder. If necessary, the pressure can be made good for any possible losses by working the hand pump.
16. After the specimen has failed or 20% strain is recorded, as the case may be (*a*) stop application of load (*b*) disconnect the chamber from water storage cylinder by closing the linger valve (*c*) open the airlock knob a little and (*d*) open the valve to drain out the water in the cylinder. After a few seconds open the airlock nut completely to facilitate quick draining out of water, by entry of air at top of the cylinder.
17. After the water is completely drained out, take out the cylinder from loading frame carefully, loosen the nuts and remove the Lucite cylinder from its base, without disturbing the sample.
18. Note the space of the failed specimen, angle of shear plane if any and dimensions of the specimen.
19. Wipe of the rubber membrane dry and find its weight W_2 that should be same as W_1.
20. Remove the membrane from the specimen and take a representative specimen preferably from the sheared zone.
21. Repeat the test with three samples of the same specimen subjected to three different lateral pressures (confining) of 0.5, 1.0 and 1.5 kg/cm^2 (5, 10 and 15psi. or 50, 100 and 150 kpa)

CALCULATIONS

1. Axial strain $= \Delta L/L$ = change in length /initial length. This is expressed as a % for convenience.
2. The stress intensity applied vertically is obtained by dividing the load, P by the cross sectional area of the specimen. At any time when axial strain is ε. Area, $A = A_o/(1-\varepsilon)$ where A_o is the initial cross sectional area of the sample. The intensity of stress = P/A. As the sample is enclosed in a rubber membrane and is sealed at either end, its volume is constant as no air or water can escape. So as the length decreases due to compression, area should increase which is assumed to be uniform. Therefore

   $A = A_o/(1-\varepsilon)$

RESULTS

1. A graph is drawn between the deviator stress and strain. The deviator stress is the difference between the stresses in axial and radial direction i.e. $(\sigma_1 - \sigma_3)$ and is equal to the vertical stress P/A. σ_3 is the lateral confining pressure at any time, which is constant for a test. From the plot, determine the second results at half the ultimate stress, which can be taken as modulus of elasticity.
2. The Mohr's circle of stress to define the state of stress at failure is drawn for each sample. The circle has for its centre point $(\sigma_1 + \sigma_3)/2$ and the radius equal to $(\sigma_1 - \sigma_3)/2$. An envelop, which approximates to a straight line, is drawn touching the circle. The intercept made on Y-axis and the slope of the envelop gives the values of strength parameters of the soil C and ϕ respectively.

DISCUSSION

In this test, the stresses considered are the total stress. As no water is allowed to escape from the specimen, effective stress parameters cannot be determined. The behaviour of a sample in this test resembles that of a fine soil in the field immediately after construction of a structure on the soil i.e. short-term strength.

TRIAXIAL TEST OBSERVATIONS

Project name & location of site:

Project report No:

Location of sample:

Sample collected on: Sample collected by:

Sample tested by: Sample tested on:

Proving ring constant:

TABLE 17.1
Triaxial test observations (stresses and strains)

TRIAL - 1

Diameter of the sample = ; Height of the sample = ;

Density of sample =

Confining pressure σ_3 =

% strain	Axial deformation (mm)	Deformation dial gauge reading	Proving ring reading	Load in Proving ring, P	Deviator stress $(\sigma_1 - \sigma_3)$ = P/A	Major principal stress, σ_1
1.0						
1.5						
2.0						
2.5						
3.0						
3.5						
4.0						
5.0						
6.0						
7.0						
8.0						
9.0						
10.0						
11.0						
12.0						
13.0						
14.0						
15.0						
16.0						
17.0						
18.0						
19.0						
20.0						

TRIAL - 2

Diameter of the sample = ; Height of the sample = ;

Density of sample =

Confining pressure σ_3 =

% strain	Axial deformation (mm)	Deformation dial gauge reading	Proving-ring reading	Load in Proving ring, P	Deviator stress $(\sigma_1 - \sigma_3)$ = P/A	Major principal stress, σ_1
1.0						
1.5						
2.0						
2.5						
3.0						
3.5						
4.0						
5.0						
6.0						
7.0						
8.0						
9.0						
10.0						
11.0						
12.0						
13.0						
14.0						
15.0						
16.0						
17.0						
18.0						
19.0						
20.0						

TRIAL - 3

Diameter of the sample = ; Height of the sample = ;

Density of sample =

Confining pressure σ_3 =

% strain	Axial deformation (mm)	Deformation dial gauge reading	Proving ring reading	Load in Proving ring, P	Deviator stress $(\sigma_1 - \sigma_3)$ = P/A	Major principal stress, σ_1
1.0						
1.5						
2.0						
2.5						
3.0						
3.5						
4.0						
5.0						
6.0						
7.0						
8.0						
9.0						
10.0						
11.0						
12.0						
13.0						
14.0						
15.0						
16.0						
17.0						
18.0						
19.0						
20.0						

TRIAL - 4

Diameter of the sample = ; Height of the sample = ;
Density of sample =

Confining pressure σ_3 =

% strain	Axial deformation (mm)	Deformation dial gauge reading	Proving ring reading	Load in Proving-ring, P	Deviator stress $(\sigma_1 - \sigma_3)$ = P/A	Major principal stress, σ_1
1.0						
1.5						
2.0						
2.5						
3.0						
3.5						
4.0						
5.0						
6.0						
7.0						
8.0						
9.0						
10.0						
11.0						
12.0						
13.0						
14.0						
15.0						
16.0						
17.0						
18.0						
19.0						
20.0						

QUESTIONS

1. How do you classify the test based on drainage conditions? Explain.
2. How do you ensure the sample is completely consolidated?
3. How do you ensure the complete drainage during shear?
4. Two samples from a pure clay soil are subjected to triaxial test at confining pressures of 50 kpa and 100 kpa. If the first sample fails at a deviator stress of 20 kpa, what would be the failure deviator stress for second sample?
5. What do you understand by effective strength parameters and total stress parameters? Which will be higher? Explain.

18

STANDARD PROCTOR COMPACTION TEST

AIM

To determine Optimum Moisture Content (OMC) and maximum dry density for a soil by conducting standard proctor compaction test.

THEORY

Compaction is the process of densification of soil mass, by reducing air voids under dynamic loading. On the other hand, though consolidation is also a process of densification of soil mass but it is due to the expulsion of water, under the action of continuously acting static load over a long period.

The degree of compaction of a soil is measured in terms of its dry density. The degree of compaction mainly depends upon its moisture content during compaction, compaction energy and the type of soil. For a given compaction energy, every soil attains the maximum dry density at a particular water content which is known as optimum moisture content (OMC).

APPLICATIONS

Compaction of soil increases its dry density, shear strength and bearing capacity. The compaction of soil decreases its void ratio, permeability and settlements. The results of this test are useful in studying the stability earthen structures like earthen dams, embankments, roads and airfields. In such constructions, the soils are compacted. The moisture content at which the soils are to be compacted in the field is estimated by the value of optimum moisture content determined by the Proctor compaction test.

APPARATUS

1. Cylindrical mould (of capacity 1000 cc, internal diameter 100 mm and height 127.3 mm).
2. Rammer (face diameter 50 mm, mass 2.6 kg, free drop 310 mm).
3. Mould accessories (detachable base plate, removable collar).
4. I.S. Sieve (20 mm, aperture).
5. Balance (10 kg. capacity).
6. Sensitive balance (least count 10 mg).
7. Graduated jar.
8. Straight edge.
9. Mixing pan (approximate size 750mm × 600mm).
10. Spatula.
11. Oven.
12. Bins.

PROCEDURE

1. Take about 20 kg of air-dried soil.
2. Sieve the soil through 20 mm sieve. Take the soil that passes through the sieve for testing.
3. Take 2.5 kg of the soil and add water to it to bring its moisture content to about 4% in coarse grained soils and 8% in case of fine grained soils.
4. Clean, dry and grease the mould and base plate. Weigh the mould with base plate. Fit the collar.
5. Compact the wet soil in three equal layers by the rammer with 25 evenly distributed blows in each layer.

6. Remove the collar and trim off the soil flush with the top of the mould. In removing the collar rotate it to break the bond between it and the soil before lifting it off the mould.
7. Clean the outside of the mould and weigh the mould with soil and base plate.
8. Remove the soil from the mould and obtain a representative soil sample from the bottom, middle and top for water content determination.
9. Repeat the above procedure with 8, 12, 16 and 20% of water contents for coarse grained soil and 14, 18, 22 and 26% for fine grained fresh soil samples approximately. The above moisture contents are given only for guidance. However, the moisture contents may be selected based on experience so that, the dry density of soil shows the increase and followed by a decrease with continuous increase in moisture content. Each trial should be performed on a fresh sample.

PRECAUTIONS

1. Adequate period (about 15minutes for clay soils and 5minutes for coarse grained soils) is allowed after mixing the water and before compacting into the mould.
2. The blows should be uniformly distributed over the surface of each layer.
3. Each layer of compacted soil is scored with a spatula before placing the soil for the succeeding layer.

OBSERVATIONS AND CALCULATIONS

1. Enter all the observations in Table 18.1 and calculate the wet density.
2. Calculate the dry density by using the equation

$$\gamma_{dry} = \gamma_{wet} / (1 + m)$$

where

γ_{dry} = dry density (g/cc)

γ_{wet} = wet density (g/cc)

m = moisture content (ratio)

3. Plot the moisture content on X-axis and dry density on Y-axis. Draw a smooth curve passing through the points, called compaction curve as shown in Fig. 18.1

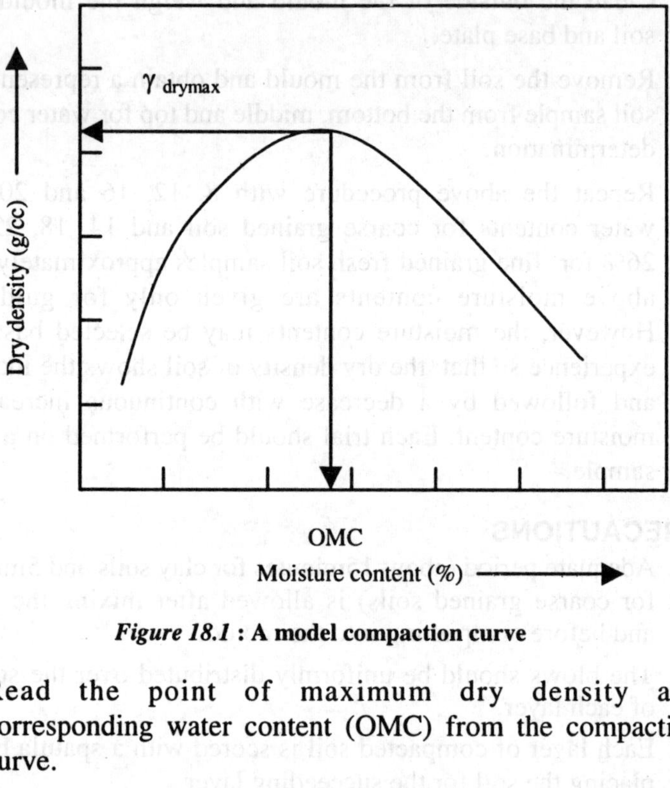

Figure 18.1 **: A model compaction curve**

4. Read the point of maximum dry density and corresponding water content (OMC) from the compaction curve.

TABLE 18.1

STANDARD PROCTOR COMPACTION TEST OBSERVATION

Project name & location of site:

Project report No:

Location of sample:

Sample collected on: Sample tested by:

Sample tested on:

Diameter of mould, d (cm) = ; Height of mould, h (cm) =

Volume of mould, v (cc) = ; Weight of the mould, w_1 (g) =

Trial Number	1	2	3	4	5
1. Weight of mould + compacted wet soil w_2 (g)					
2. Weight of compacted soil w = $w_2 - w_1$ (g)					
3. Wet density of soil γ_{wet} = w/v (g/cc)					
4. Bin Number					
5. Empty weight of bin (g)					
6. Weight of bin + wet soil (g)					
7. Weight of bin + dry soil (g)					
8. Weight of water (6) – (7) (g)					
9. Weight of dry soil (7) – (5) (g)					
10. Moisture content, m (8)/(9)					
11. m (%) = m × 100					
12. Dry density (γ_{wet}) /(1 + m) (g/cc)					

RESULT

Optimum Moisture Content, OMC (%) =

Maximum dry density (g/cc) =

QUESTIONS

1. What is compaction of soil? Why it is done?
2. Differentiate between compaction and consolidation of soils?
3. What is optimum moisture content?
4. What is maximum dry density of soil at its OMC? Does it mean that density cannot be more than this, for a given soil?
5. What is meant by dry side and wet side of optimum moisture content? Which side is preferred for field compaction? Explain.
6. What do you understand by field compaction control?
7. How does laboratory compaction results help in the control of field compaction?

8. What are the soil properties affected by compaction?
9. Are the optimum moisture content and maximum dry density are constants for one type of soil? Explain.
10. What are the field applications of compaction test?
11. Why is it called Proctor compaction test?
12. What are the approximate values of optimum moisture content and dry density for coarse grained and fine grained soils?
13. Differentiate between standard Proctor compaction and modified Proctor compaction test?
14. How do you obtain the same compaction efforts in the field?

19

DETERMINATION OF RELATIVE DENSITY (Dr) OF COHESIONLESS SOILS

AIM

To determine the relative density of cohesionless soil.

THEORY AND APPLICATION

Relative density is also known as density index. It is defined as the ratio of difference between the void ratio of a cohesionless soil in the loosest state and any given void ratio to the difference between its void ratios in the loosest and in the densest states. For cohesionless soils in the natural or artificially compacted states neither the actual density (or void ratio) nor the actual density expressed as a percentage of the maximum density give an exact idea of the compactness of the soil. The concept of density index (relative density) gives a practically useful measure of compactness of such soils. The compactive characteristics of cohesionless soils and the related properties of such soils are dependent on factors like grain size distribution and shape of individual particles. Relative density is also effected by these factors and serve as a parameter to correlate properties of soils. Various soil properties, such as penetration resistance, compressibility, compaction, friction angle, permeability and California bearing ratio has been found to have simple relationships with relative density. Density index is also used to asses the possibility of a soil to fail under liquefaction.The Tables 19.1 and 19.2 gives some of the properties as a function of relative density.

TABLE 19.1

Empirical values of ϕ, N-value and compactness of soil as a function of relative density (source, Bowles. 1982)

Relative density, D_r (%)	Compactness of soil	Penetration resistance (N-value)	Approximate angle of internal friction, ϕ (degrees)
15	Very loose to loose	5-10	27-32
35	Loose to medium	8-15	30-35
65	Medium to dense	10-40	35-40
85	Dense to very dense	20-70	38-43
100	Very dense	>35	-

TABLE 19.2

Approximate relationship between earthquake magnitude, D_r (%), and liquefaction potential for water table 1.5m below ground surface (source: Seed and Idriss, 1971; cited by Bowles, 1982)

Earthquake acceleration	D_r — causing high liquefaction probability	D_r — Providing stability against liquefaction
0.10g	< 33	> 54
0.15g	< 48	> 73
0.20g	< 60	> 85
0.25g	< 70	> 92

APPARATUS

1. **Vibratory table:** A steel table with a cushioned steel vibrating deck about 75 × 75 cm. The vibrator should have a net weight of over 45 kg. The vibrator should have frequency of 3600 vibrations per minute, a vibrator amplitude variable between 0.05 and 0.65 mm under a 115 kg load.
2. **Moulds:** Cylindrical metal density moulds of 3000 cc (150 mm dia. and 169.77 mm high) and 15000 cc (280 mm dia. and 243.6 mm high) capacity.

3. One guide sleeve with clamp assembly should be provided with lock nuts.
4. One 10 mm thick surcharge base plate, with handle, for each mould.
5. **Surcharge weights:** One surcharge weight for each size mould. The total weight of surcharge base plate and surcharge weight shall be equivalent to 140 g/cm^2 for the mould being used.
6. One dial gauge holder.
7. **Dial gauge:** A dial gauge with 50mm travel and 0.02mm least count.
8. A metallic calibration bar of size 75 × 300 × 3 mm.
9. **Pouring devices:** Consisting of funnels 12 mm and 25 mm in diameter and 150 mm long, with cylindrical spots and lipped brims for attaching to 150mm and 300 mm high metal cans.
10. **Mixing pans:** Two mixing pans. Suitable sizes are, one 60 × 90 cm and 10 cm deep and 40 × 40 cm and 5 cm deep.
11. **Weighing scale:** Portable platform scale, 100kg capacity with sensitivity of 20g.
12. Hoist of at least 135kg capacity.
13. Metal hand scoop.
14. Bristled brush.
15. Stop watch.
16. Metal straight edge 40 cm long.
17. Micrometer: 0 to 25 mm with an accuracy of 0.025 mm.

TEST PROCEDURE

The test procedure to determine the relative density of soil involves the measurement of density of soil in its loosest possible state (γ_{min}) and densest possible states (γ_{max}). Knowing the specific gravity of soil solids (G_s) the void ratios of the soil in its loosest (e_{max}) and densest state (e_{min}) are computed. The density of soil in the field (γ) (natural state) is used to compute the void ratio (e) in the field. After obtaining the three void ratios (i.e. Minimum, maximum and natural) the relative density is computed. To measure the densities depending on the particle sizes one of the two moulds (3000 cc or 15000 cc) are used as presented in Table 19.3. Hence these moulds have to be initially calibrated. Then the possible minimum and maximum densities of the soil are obtained as explained below.

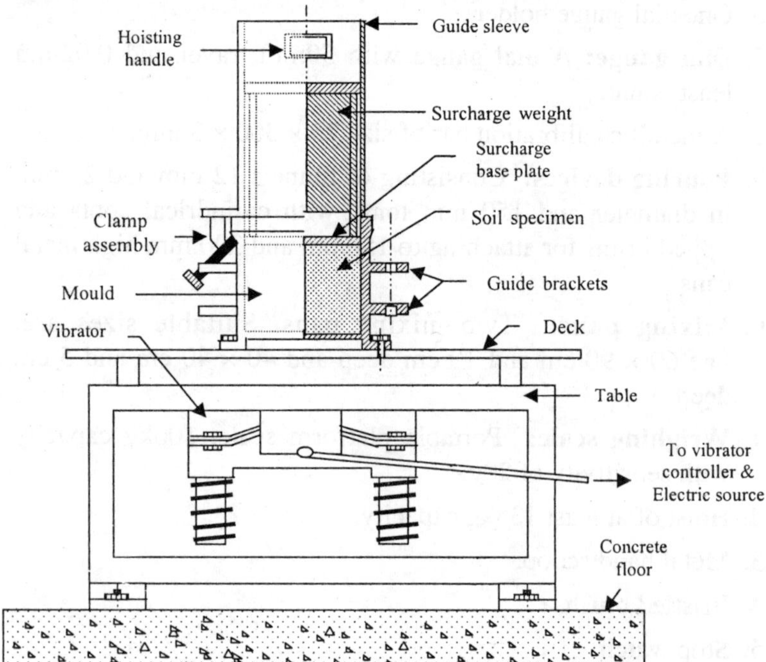

Figure 19.1 **: Assembly of the relative density test apparatus**

CALIBRATION OF MOULDS

To calibrate, the mould should be filled with water and a glass plate should be slide carefully over the top surface of the mould in such a manner as to ensure that the mould is completely filled with water. The volume of the mould should be calculated in cc by dividing the weight of water in the mould by the unit weight of water.

PREPARATION OF SOIL SAMPLE

A representative sample of soil should be selected. The weight of soil sample to be taken depends upon the maximum size of particles in the soil as given in Table 19.3. The soil sample should be dried in an oven at a temperature of 105° to 110°C. The soil sample should be pulverized without breaking the individual soil particles and sieved through the required sieve.

TABLE 19.3

Weight of soil sample to be taken for the test (as per IS: 2720 , Part XIV)

Maximum size of soil particle (mm)	Weight of soil sample required (kg)	Pouring device to be used in the test for the determination of minimum density	Size of mould to be used (cc)
80	45	Shovel or large scoop	15000
40	12	Scoop	3000
20	12	Scoop	3000
10	12	Pouring device (25 mm dia spout)	3000
4.75	12	Pouring device (12 mm dia spout)	3000

Procedure for the determination of Minimum density

1. The pouring device and mould should be selected according to the maximum size of particle as indicated in Table 19.3. The mould should be weighed and weight recorded. Oven-dry soil should be used.

2. Soil containing particles samaller than 10 mm should be placed as loosely as possible in the mould by pouring the soil through the spout in a steady stream. The spout should be adjused so that the height of free fall of the soil is always 25mm. While pouring the soil the pouring device should be moved in a spiral motion from the outside towards the centre to form a soil layer of uniform thickness without segregation. The mould should be filled approximately 25 mm above the top and levelled with the

top by making one continuous pass with the steel straight edge. If all excess material is not removed, an additional continuous pass should be made. Great care shall be exercised to avoid jarring during the entire pouring and trimming operation.

3. The mould and the soil should be weighed and the weight recorded.
4. Soil containing particles larger than 10mm should be placed by means of a large scoop (or shovel) held as close as possible to and just above the soil surface to cause the material to slide rather than fall into the previously placed soil. If necessary, large particles may be held by hand to prevent them from rolling off the scoop. The mould should be filled to overflowing but not more than 25 mm above the top. The surface of the soil should be levelled with the top of the mould using the steel straight edge in such a way that any slight projections of the larger particles above the top of the mould shall approximately balance the large voids in the surface below the top of the mould. The mould and the soil should be weighed and the weight recorded.

Procedure for the determination of maximum density

The maximum density of soil may be determined by either the dry or wet method.

DRY METHOD

1. The guide sleeve should be assembled on top of the mould and the clamp assemblies tightened so that the inner surfaces of the walls of the mould and the sleeve are in line. The lock nuts should be tightened. The third clamp should be loosened, the guide sleeve removed, the empty mould weighed and its weight recorded.
2. The mould should then be filled with the thoroughly mixed oven dry soil in a loose state (The mould filled for the determination of minimum density may also be used for this test).
3. The guide sleeves should be attached to the mould and the surcharge base plate should be placed on the soil surface. The surcharge weight should then be lowered on to the base plate using the hoist in the case of the 15000 cc mould.

4. The mould should be fixed to the vibrator deck. The assembly of mould fixed on to the vibrating table is shown in the Fig. 19.1. The vibrator control should be set at its maximum amplitude and the loaded soil specimen should be vibrated for 8 minutes.
5. The surcharge weight and the guide sleeves should be removed from the mould. The dial gauge readings on two opposite sides of the surcharge base plate should be obtained and the average recorded. The mould with the soil should be weighed and its weight recorded.

WET METHOD

1. The wet method may be conducted on dry soil or wet soil from the field.
2. The mould should be filled with wet soil. Sufficient water should be added to the soil to allow a small quantity of free water to accumulate on the surface of the soil during filling. During and just after filling the mould, it should be vibrated for a total of six minutes. During this period the amplitude of the vibrator should be reduced as much as necessary to avoid excessive boiling and fluffing of the soil, which may occur in some soils. During the final minutes of vibration, any water appearing above the surface of the soil should be removed.
3. The guide sleeve, surcharge base plate and surcharge weight should be assembled as described in dry method.
4. The specimen with the surcharge weight, should be vibrated for 8 minutes. After the vibration, the surcharge weight and the guide should be removed from the mould. Dial gauge reading should be obtained on two opposite sides of the base plate and recorded. The entire wet specimen should be carefully removed from the mould, dried to contant weight, weighed and the weight recorded.

OBSERVATIONS AND CALCULATIONS

The Minimum density test observations are recorded in Table 19.4 and the maximum density test results are tabulated in Table 19.5. Table 19.6 shows the computation steps for relative density.

TABLE 19.4

Observations for the determination of minimum density

Project:
Details of soil sample:

Tested by:

Mould No.
Weight of the mould: Volume of the mould:
Method used: Funnel/Scoop Size of mould:

Test No.	1	2	3
Weight of mould, g			
Weight of soil + mould, g			
Weight of soil, W, g			
Calibrated volume of mould, V_c, cc			
Minimum density, $\gamma_{min} = W / V_c$, g/cc			

TABLE 19.5

Observations for the determination of maximum density

Project:
Details of soil sample: Tested by:
Mould No.
Weight of mould, in g: Volume of mould V_c, in cc:
Dial gauge reading at left: Dial gauge reading at right:
Average dial gauge reading:
Method used: Dry/Wet Size of mould:

Test No.	1	2	3
Gauge reading : Left			
Right			
Average gauge reading, D_f			
Initial gauge reading, D_i			
Surface area of soil sample, A, cm^2			
Volume of soil $V_s = V_c - (D_i - D_f)A$, cc			
Weight of dry soil + mould, g			
Weight of dry soil, W, g			
Maximum density $\gamma_{max} = W/ V_s$, g/cc			

TABLE 19.6

Computation of relative density

Test No.	1	2	3
In-place density, γ_d, g/cc			
γ_{max}, g/cc			
γ_{min}, g/cc			
$\gamma_d - \gamma_{min}$			
$\gamma_{max} - \gamma_{min}$			
Relative density, (%)			
$D_r = (\gamma_{max})(\gamma_d - \gamma_{min})/$ $\{\gamma_d(\gamma_{max} - \gamma_{min})\} \times 100$			
In-place moisture content of soil, (%)			

RESULTS

Maximum density, g/cc =

Minimum density, g/cc =

Relative density (%) =

20

CALIFORNIA BEARING RATIO (CBR) TEST

AIM

To determine the California Bearing Ratio (CBR) value for the given soil.

THEORY AND APPLICATION

CBR is the ratio of the force per unit area required to penetrate a soil mass with a standard circular piston of 1875(mm^2) cross sectional area at the rate of 1.25mm/minute to that required sample of compacted stone was defined as having a CBR of 100%.

The standard load (Ps) corresponding to 2.5mm penetration of the plunger into the standard sample is reported to be 1370kg and for 5mm penetration it was found to be 2055kg.

California bearing ratio values are useful in estimating the thickness of flexible pavements. Based on the CBR values of subgrade and on the traffic volume expected on the road one can design the thickness of flexible pavement.

APPARATUS

1. Loading frame.
2. CBR mould (150mm diameter and 175 mm height).
3. Annular weights each of 2.5 kg.
4. Hammer having a weight of 4.89kg with a drop of 450mm.
5. Spacer disc 50 mm height, 150 mm diameter.

6. Tray to mix soil.
7. Measuring jar.
8. Balance (20kg capacity).

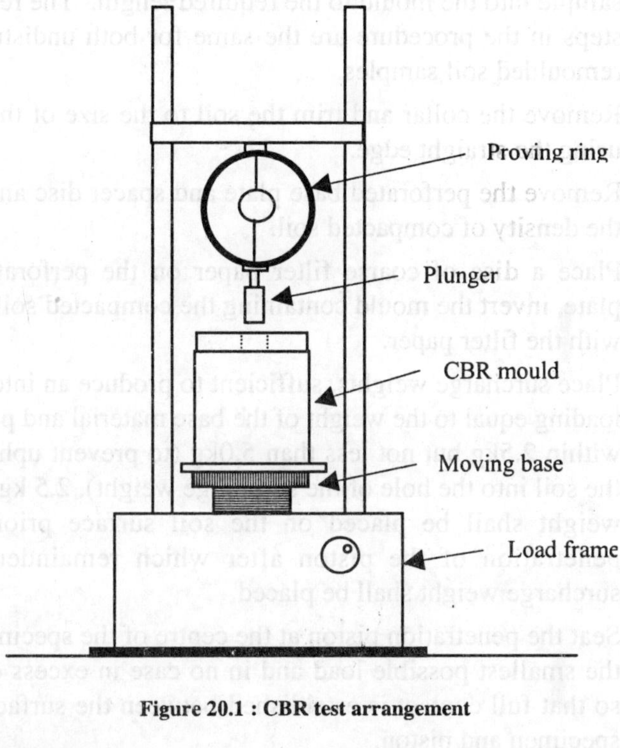

Figure 20.1 : CBR test arrangement

PROCEDURE

1. Take 4.5kg of oven dry soil sample and add required quantity of water (so as to obtain OMC) to the soil and mix it thoroughly.
2. Fit the cylindrical mould with an extension collar and perforated base plate and apply a thin film of oil to the inside faces of the mould, base plate and the collar.
3. Insert the spacer disc over the base plate and place a 150mm diameter coarse filter paper on top of the disc.
4. The well mixed soil (preferably cured for 24 hours in a

container with air tight cover) is then compacted in the prepared mould in five layers and each layer receives 55 blows of the specified rammer. If the undisturbed soil sample has to be tested, transfer the 150 mm diameter core sample into the mould to the required length. The remaining steps in the procedure are the same for both undisturbed or remoulded soil samples.

5. Remove the collar and trim the soil to the size of the mould using the straight edge.
6. Remove the perforated base plate and spacer disc and obtain the density of compacted soil.
7. Place a disc of coarse filter paper on the perforated base plate, invert the mould containing the compacted soil contact with the filter paper.
8. Place surcharge weights, sufficient to produce an intensity of loading equal to the weight of the base material and pavement within 2.5kg but not less than 5.0kg (to prevent upheaval of the soil into the hole of the surcharge weight), 2.5 kg annular weight shall be placed on the soil surface prior to the penetration of the piston after which remainder of the surcharge weight shall be placed.
9. Seat the penetration piston at the centre of the specimen with the smallest possible load and in no case in excess of 4.5kg so that full contact is established between the surface of the specimen and piston.
10. By choosing a suitable position for the regulating value on the hydraulic pressure unit, apply the loads on the penetration piston so that the rate of application is 1.25mm/minute.
11. Load readings shall be recorded at plunger penetration values of 0, 0.5, 1.0, 1.5, 2.0, 2.5, 3.0, 4.0, 5.0, 7.5, 10.0 and 12.5mm as shown in Table 20.1.
12. After taking the readings, unload the specimen, and detach the mould from the loading frame.
13. Collect about 50g of soil sample from the top 30mm layer of the specimen and determine the moisture content.

OBSERVATIONS AND CALCULATIONS

TABLE 20.1

OBSERVATIONS OF CBR TEST

Project name & location of site:

Project report No:

Location of sample:

Sample collected on: ; Sample tested by:

Diameter of mould, d (cm) = ; Height of mould, h (cm) =

Volume of mould, v (cc) = ; Weight of mould, w_1(g) =

Least count of penetration dial gauge = ; Proving ring constant =

Penetration dial gauge	Penetrati - on (mm)	Proving ring reading	Load (kg)	Corrected load (kg)
	0.0			
	0.5			
	1.0			
	1.5			
	2.0			
	2.5			
	3.0			
	4.0			
	5.0			
	7.5			
	10.0			
	12.5			

A load-penetration curve shall be plotted (penetration on the X-axis and load on Y-axis). This shall be mainly convex upwards. However, due to surface irregularities of the sample sometimes the initial portion of the curve may be concave upwards. A correction shall then be applied by drawing a tangent to the curve at the point of greatest slope. The corrected curve shall be taken to be this tangent plus the convex portion of the original curve with the origin of penetration shifted to the point where the tangent cuts the horizontal axis as shown in Fig. 20.2.

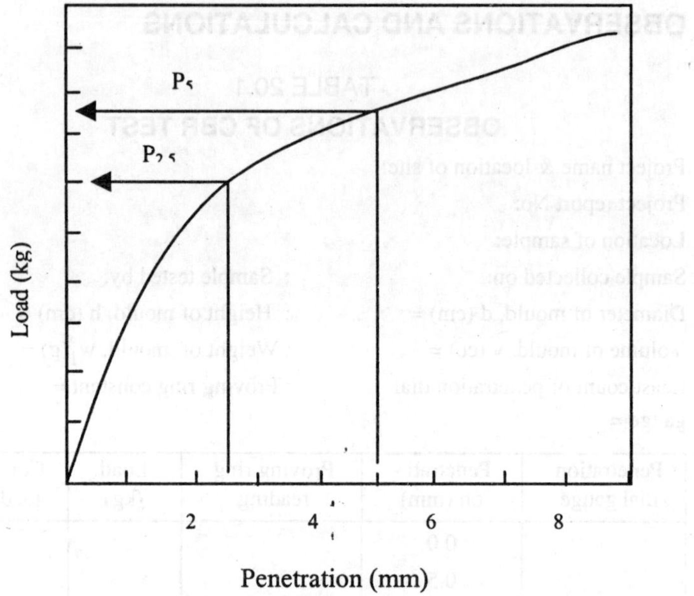

(a) Curve needing no correction

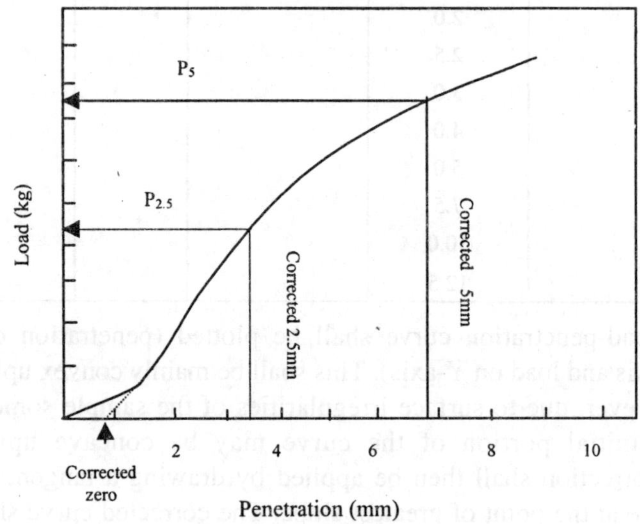

(b) Curve needing correction

Figure 20.2 **: General pattern of CBR load-penetration curves**

BEARING RATIO

California bearing ratio is generally estimated corresponding to 2.5mm and 5mm penetration of the plunger. To estimate CBR value at 2.5mm penetration: let the corrected load corresponding to 2.5mm penetration be $P_{2.5}$ (i.e. the 2.5mm penetration has to be measured from the corrected zero). The standard load ($P_{s2.5}$) corresponding to this penetration, as explained earlier, is 1370 kg.

Then $CBR_{2.5} = P2.5 / P_{s2.5}$

Similarly $CBR_5 = P_5 / P_{s5}$

Where $P_{s5} = 2055$kg.

RESULT

CBR value of soil sample shall be reported correct to the first decimal place.

QUESTIONS

1. Why is it called bearing ratio?
2. What are the standard loads? Explain.
3. What is the field application of CBR value?
4. What is the rate of penetration of plunger recommended for CBR test?

21

DETERMINATION OF WATER CONTENT-DRY DENSITY RELATIONSHIP USING HEAVY COMPACTION TEST

AIM

To determine Optimum Moisture Content (OMC) and maximum dry density for a soil by conduction of heavy compaction test.

THEORY

The standard Proctor (light) compaction method of determining OMC and maximum dry density was developed by Proctor in1933 by considering the field compaction equipment available then which gave a relatively low density. As field compaction equipment became heavier and more efficient it became necessary to increase the amount of compacting energy in the laboratory test. This has resulted in the standard test with heavier compaction. This procedure is satisfactory for cohesive soils but does not lend itself well to the study of the compaction characteristics of clean sand or gravel, which displace easily when struck with the rammer.

APPARATUS

1. **Cylindrical metal mould:** of volume either 1000 cc (100 mm diameter and 127.3 mm height) or 2250cc (150 mm diameter and 127.3mm height). The mould shall be fitted with a detachable base-plate and a removable extension approximately 60 mm high.

2. **Metal rammer:** It shall have a 50 mm diameter circular face, and weigh 4.89 kg. The rammer should be equipped with a suitable arrangement for controlling the drop to the specified amount of 450 mm.
3. Sample extruder for the purpose of extruding compacted specimens from the mould.
4. **Balance:** one, of capacity 10 kg sensitive to 1g and another of capacity 200 g sensitive to 0.01 g.
5. Oven.
6. Bins for moisture content determinations.
7. **Sieves:** of aperture size 20 mm and 4.75 mm.
8. **Tray :** of size 90 cm × 60 cm.
9. Mixing tools.
10. **Trimming tools:** Spatula, knife etc.

PROCEDURE

1. Preparation of soil specimen:

A representative soil sample weighing about 20kg or more of the thoroughly mixed air dried soil is obtained. The sample is made to pass through 20 mm and 4.75 mm sieves, separating the fractions retained and passing these seives. Care shall be exercised so as not to break the aggregate while pulverizing. The percentage of each fraction shall be determined. The fraction retained on 20 mm sieve shall not be used in the test. The percentage of soil coarser than 4.75 mm sieve and the percentage of soil coarser than 20 mm sieve shall be determined.

The ratio of fraction passing 20 mm sieve and retained on 4.75 mm sieve to the soil passing 4.75 mm sieve shall be determined. The material retained on and passing 4.75mm sieve shall be mixed thoroughly in the calculated proportion to obtain about 16 to 18 kg of soil specimen. (In case the material passing 20 mm sieve and retained on 4.75mm sieve is more than 20 percent, the ratio of such material to the material passing 4.75 mm sieve shall be maintained for each determination in a test. If the coarse material retained on 4.75 mm sieve is less than 20 percent the sample passing the 20 mm sieve may be directly used.)

2. Take about 16 kg of the soil specimen prepared as explained above. Enough water shall be added to the specimen to bring its moisture content to about 7% (sandy soils) and 10% (clayey soils) less than the estimated optimum moisture content. The processed soil shall be kept in an air-tight tin for about 18 to 20 hours to ensure thoroughly mixing of the water with soil.
3. Take about 3kg of water mixed soil, if 1000cc mould is used and about 8kg if 2250cc mould is used. Wet soil shall be compacted into the mould in five equal layers, each layer being given 25 blows if the 1000cc mould is used or 56 blows. If the 2250cc mould is used from the rammer weighing 4.89 kg dropping from a height of 450 mm. Each layer of the compacted soil shall be scored with a spatula before putting the soil for the succeeding layer.
4. The collar shall then be removed and the compacted soil shall be carefully levelled off to the top of the mould by means of straight edge. The mould and the soil shall be weighed to the nearest 1g.
5. The soil shall be ejected out of the mould, cut in the middle and a representative soil specimen shall be taken for moisture content determination.
6. The procedure shall be repeated five to six times using the fresh part of the soil specimen and after adding a higher water content than the preceding specimen, so that at least two readings each below and above optimum moisture content are available. Calculate the wet density of soil. Assuming that the moisture content added to the soil is equal to the actual moisture content (actual moisture content will be more than the added moisture content by an amount equal to the absorbed moisture content) calculate the dry density of the compacted soil in each trial. Plot a graph between the approximate moisture content to dry density of soil. The curve indicates that as the moisture content is increased the γ_{dry} initially increases and reaches a maximum then it decreases with further increase in moisture content.

OBSERVATIONS AND CALCULATIONS

1. **Wet density:** The wet density of the compacted soil shall be calculated as follows:

$$\gamma_{wet} = (W - W_m)/V$$

where

γ_{wet} = wet density of compacted soil,

W = weight of mould with wet compacted soil,

W_m = weight of empty mould,

V = volume of mould.

2. **Dry density:** The dry density of compacted soil shall be calculated as follows:

$$\gamma_{dry} = \gamma_{wet}/(1 + m)$$

where

γ_{dry} = dry density of soil,

γ_{wet} = wet density of soil,

m = moisture content, (ratio)

Correction for oversize fraction

If the material retained on 20mm sieve (or 4.75mm sieve) has been excluded from the test, the following correction shall be applied for getting the values of maximum dry density and optimum moisture content for the total soil. For this purpose, the specific gravity of the portion retained and passing the 20mm sieve or 4.75mm sieve, as the case may be, should be determined separately:

Correction for maximum dry density $= \gamma_s \gamma_{drymax}/(n_1 \gamma_{drymax} + n_2 \gamma_s)$

Corrected optimum moisture content $= n_1 A_o + n_2 m_o$

where

γ_s = unit weight of the oversize gravel particles in g/cc (= G γ_s ; G = specific gravity of gravel particles)

γ_{drymax} = maximum dry density obtained in the test in g/cc

n_1 = fraction by weight of the oversize particles in the total soil expressed as ratio.

n_2 = fraction by weight of the portion passing 20 mm sieve (or 4.75mm sieve) expressed as ratio of total soil.

A_o = water absorption capacity of oversize material, if any expressed as percentage of water absorbed.

m_o = optimum moisture content observed in the test.

TABLE 21.1

Heavy compaction test data

Name of the Project : Location:

Sample No.: Volume of mould:

Weight of the rammer: Fall of the rammer:

Specific gravity

Percentage of material:

1. Retained on 20mm sieve
2. Passing 20mm sieve and retained on 4.75mm sieve
3. Passing 4.75mm sieve

Ratio of (2) to (3)

Tested by

Density Observations

Trial No.		1	2	3	4	5	6
Weight of mould + compacted soil	(g)						
Weight of mould	(g)						
Weight of compacted wet soil	(g)						
Wet density	(g/cc)						
Water content (m)	(%)						
Dry density	(g/cc)						
Void ratio							
Porosity							

Water content Observations

Trial No.		1	2	3	4	5	6	7
Bin No.								
Weight of Bin + wet soil	(g)							
Weight of Bin + dry soil	(g)							
Weight of water	(g/cc)							
Weight of Bin	(g/cc)							
Water content (m)	(%)							

RESULTS

Optimum moisture content (observed) =

Maximum dry density (observed) =

Optimum moisture content (corrected) =

Maximum dry density (corrected) =

22

DETERMINATION OF LINEAR SHRINKAGE IN SOILS

AIM

To determine the linear shrinkage of remoulded soils.

APPARATUS

1. Two palette knives.
2. Flat grass plate (approximately 10mm thick and 45cm square or an evaporating dish approximately 15cm diameter).
3. Mould of cast iron or brass (as shown in Fig. 22.1).
4. Oven
5. Vernier gauge to measure 15cm
6. Grease

PROCEDURE

1. The mould shall be thoroughly cleaned and a thin film of grease shall then be applied to its inner walls in order to prevent the soil from adhering to the mould.
2. About 150g of the soil sample passing through 425μ sieve shall be placed on the flat glass plate and thoroughly mixed with distilled water, using the palette knives, until the mass becomes a smooth homogeneous paste, with a moisture content approximately 2% above the liquid limit. In case of clayey soils, the soil paste shall be left to stand for a sufficient time (24 hours) to allow the moisture to permeate throughout the soil mass.
3. The thoroughly mixed soil paste shall be placed in the mould

such that it is slightly proud of the sides of the mould.

4. The mould is then be gently jarred to remove any air-pockets in the paste. The soil shall then be placed so that the soil paste can air-dry slowly, until the soil has shrunk away from the walls of the mould.
5. Drying should then be completed first at a temperature of 60°C to 65°C until shrinkage has largely ceased and then at 105°C to 110°C to complete the drying.
6. The mould and the soil then be cooled and the mean length of the soil bar is measured. If the specimen has become curved during drying, the measurement should be made along the mean arc.
7. At least three determinations of linear shrinkage of the same soil shall be made and the average is taken.

PRECAUTIONS

1. The moisture content of the soil-water mixture at approximately 2% above the liquid limit of the soil is not critical to within a few percent.
2. The soil-water mixture should not be wet enough to allow segregation of the larger particles to the bottom of the mould.
3. With soils of low plasticity or shrinkage where there is no danger of cracking due to rapid drying the moulds may be placed immediately in the high temperature oven.
4. Should a specimen crack badly, or break, such that measurement is difficult, the test should be repeated at a slower drying rate.

CALCULATIONS AND REPORT

The linear shrinkage of the soil shall be calculated as a percentage of the original length of the specimen from the following formula:

$$\text{Linear shrinkage} = \{1 - L_1/L_2\} \times 100 \text{ percent}$$

where

L_1 = Length of oven dry specimen

L_2 = Initial length of specimen

The linear shrinkage of the soil shall be reported to the nearest whole number.

23

DETERMINATION OF SWELLING PRESSURE OF SOILS-CONSOLIDOMETER METHOD

AIM

To determine the swelling pressure of soils.

THEORY AND APPLICATIONS

Swelling pressure may be defined as the pressure, which the expansive soil exerts, if the soil is not allowed to swell or the volume change of the soil is arrested. The expansive clays increase in their volume when they come in contact with water owing to surface properties of these clay types. Light structures founded on these types of soils, popularly known in India as black cotton soil, experience severe structural damage due to swelling of the subsoil. Since the intrinsic swelling pressure is to be associated with the design of structures against such damages, measurement of swelling pressure assumes importance.

The swelling pressure is dependent upon several factors. They are: (*a*) the type and amount of clay in the soil and the nature of clay mineral, (*b*) the initial water content and dry density, (*c*) the nature of pore fluid, (*d*) the stress history of the soil including the confining pressure and (*e*) drying and wetting cycles to which the soils have been subjected to. Besides, the dependence of swelling pressure on volume change makes a precise measurement of swelling pressure difficult.

APPARATUS AND EQUIPMENT

1. **Consolidometer:** A device to hold the soil sample in a ring either fixed or floating with porous stones on each face of the sample (see Fig. 12.1). A consolidometer shall also provide means for submerging the sample, for applying a vertical load and for measuring the change in the thickness of the specimen with the help of a dial gauge.

2. Specimen diameter shall be 60mm (specimen of diameter 50, 70 and 100 mm may also be used in special case).

3. Specimen thickness shall be at least 20mm. However, the thickness shall not be less than 10 times the maximum diameter of the grain in the soil specimen. The diameter to thickness ratio shall be a minimum of 3.

4. Ring shall be made of a material which is non corrosive. The inner surface shall be highly polished or coated with a thin coating of silicon grease. The ring shall have one edge beveled suitably so that the sample is pressed into the ring with least disturbance.

5. Two porous stones are required. The diameter of the porous stone shall be 0.2 to 0.5 mm less than the internal diameter of the ring. The thickness of the stone shall be a minimum of 15 mm.

6. A dial gauge with an accuracy of 0.01mm and a traverse of at least 20 mm.

7. Water reservoir to keep the soil sample submerged.

8. **Soil trimming tools :** Fine wire-saw, knife, spatula, etc.

9. Thermostatically controlled oven to maintain the temperature between 105° C and 110° C.

10. Dessicator with desiccating agent.

11. Balance having a sensitivity of 0.01 g.

12. Bins for moisture content determination.

PREPARATION OF TEST SPECIMEN

Preparation of the specimen from undisturbed soil sample

1. Clean the container ring and find its empty weight.
2. Cut about 30 mm of the sample from one end of the undisturbed soil sample.
3. Insert gradually the consolidation ring in the soil sample cut by pressing with hands and carefully removing the material around the ring.
4. Trim the specimen smooth and flush with the top and bottom of the ring.
5. Any voids in the specimen caused due to removal of gravel or lime stone pieces, shall be filled back by pressing lightly the loose soil in the voids.
6. Wipe clearly any soil sticking outside the container ring and weigh the ring with the soil.

Preparation of the specimen from disturbed soil sample

1. In case where it is necessary to use disturbed soil samples, compact the soil sample to the desired density and moisture content in a standard Proctors' compaction mould.
2. Samples of the suitable size are cut from it.
3. The other procedure is same as in the case of undisturbed soil sample.

TEST PROCEDURE

1. Saturate the porous stones by boiling in distilled water for at least 15 minutes. Moisten all surfaces of the consolidometer which are to be enclosed.
2. Assemble consolidometer with the soil specimen (in the ring) and porous stones at top and bottom of the specimen, providing a filter paper rendered wet between the soil specimen and the porous stone.
3. Position the loading block centrally on the top porous stone.
4. Mount this assembly on the loading frame such that, the

load when applied is transmitted axially to the soil specimen through the loading cap.

5. Fix the holder with the dial gauge to record the progressive vertical heave of the specimen under no load and adjusted in such a way that the dial gauge is near the end of its release run, allowing small margin for the compression of the soil, if any.
6. Apply an initial setting load of 0.05kg/cm^2 and the initial reading of the dial gauge shall be noted.
7. Connect the system to a water reservoir with the level of water in the reservoir being at about the same level as the soil specimen and water allowed to flow in the sample. The soil is then allowed to swell.
8. Record at different time intervals the free swell readings shown by the dial gauge under the seating load of 0.05kg/cm^2. (Table 23.1)
9. Record the readings in Table 23.1 where the time refers to total elapsed time since starting of the initial reading.
10. Take the dial gauge readings till equilibrium is reached. This is ensured by making a plot of swelling dial reading versus time in hours, which plot becomes asymptotic with abscissa (time scale). The equilibrium of swelling is normally reached over a period of 6 to 7 days in general for all expansive soils.
11. Apply the compressive pressures on the swollen soil sample as per Table 23.2.
12. Record the compression dial readings till the dial readings attain a steady state for each load applied over the specimen.
13. Apply the consolidation loads till the specimen attains its original volume (i.e. attaining initial reading in the dial gauge).

TABLE 23.1

Swelling pressure test by consolidation method (observations during swelling)

Project: Dated: Tested by:

1. Details of soil sample
   - (i) Location
   - (ii) Bore hole No. Depth
   - (iii) Visual description of soil
   - (iv) Liquid limit: Plasticity index
   - (v) Percentage of soil fraction below 0.002mm
2. Details of soil specimen
   - (i) Undisturbed or remoulded
   - (ii) Specific gravity of the soil
   - (iii) Moisture content (%)
   - (iv) Dry density (g/cc)

Date: Time of Sarting

Elapsed time hours	Swelling dial reading
0	
0.5	
1	
2	
4	
8	
12	
16	
20	
24	
36	
48	
60	
72	
96	
120	
144	

TABLE 23.2

Swelling pressure test by consolidation method (observations during compression)

Pressure Increment		Compression (dial reading)	Change in thickness of expanded specimen (mm)
in kg/cm2	in kPa		
(0.0-0.5)	0-5		
(0.05-0.10)	5-10		
(0.10-0.25)	10-25		
(0.25-0.50)	25-50		
0.50-1.00)	50-100		
(1.00-2.00)	100-200		
(2.00-4.00)	200-400		
(4.00-8.00)	400-800		
(8.00-16.00)	800-1600		

CALCULATIONS AND REPORT

The observed swelling dial readings recorded in Table 23.1 shall be plotted with elapsed time as abscissa and the swelling dial reading as ordinates on natural scale. A smooth curve shall be drawn joining these points. If the curve so drawn becomes asymptotic with the abscissa, the swelling has reached its maximum and hence the swelling phase shall be stopped, and the consolidation phase shall be started.

The compression readings shall be tabulated in Table 23.2 and a plot of change in thickness of expanded specimen as ordinates and consolidation pressure applied as abscissa in semi-logarithmic scale shall be made. The swelling pressure exerted by the soil specimen under zero swelling condition shall be obtained by interpolation and expressed in kg/cm^2 (kPa).

RESULT

Swelling pressure =

24

DETERMINATION OF SWELLING PRESSURE OF SOILS:CONSTANT VOLUME METHOD

AIM

To determine the swelling pressure of soils.

APPARATUS AND EQUIPMENT

1. **Consolidometer :** A device to hold the sample in a ring either fixed or floating with porous stones on each face of the sample (as explained in Chapter Twenty Three).
2. **Dial gauge:** a least count of 0.002 mm with a traverse of atleast 10 mm.
3. Soil trimming tools.
4. Balance (sensitive to 0.01 g).
5. Oven (Thermostatically controlled to maintain temperature between 105° C to 110° C).
6. Desiccator
7. Moisture content Bins.
8. Loading unit of 5000 kg Capacity - Strain controlled type.
9. High sensitive proving ring of 200 kg capacity.

PREPARATION OF SOIL SPECIMEN

Preparation of specimen from undisturbed soil sample and from disturbed soil sample (as explained in Chapter Twenty Three).

PROCEDURE

1. Keep the consolidation specimen ring with the specimen in between two porous stones saturated in boiling water providing a filter paper between the soil specimen and the porous stone.
2. Position the loading block centrally on top of the porous stone.
3. Place this assembly on the platen of the loading unit as shown in Fig. 24. 1.

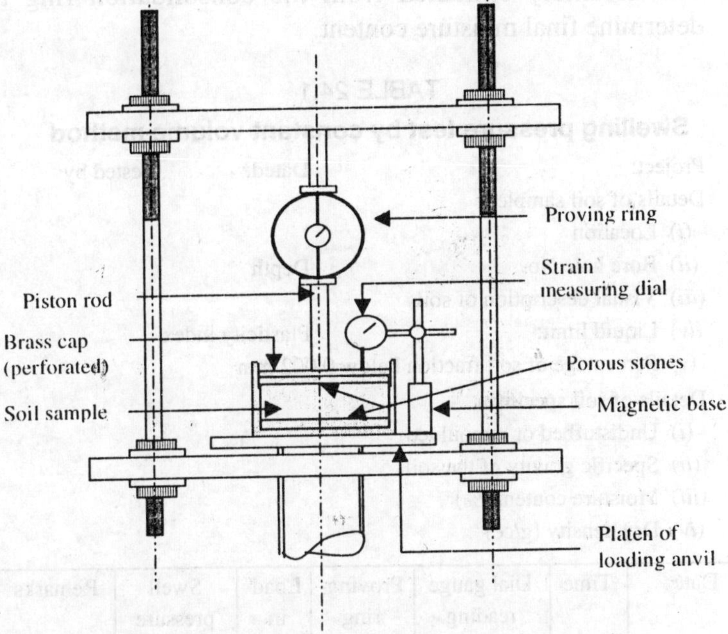

Figure 24.1 **: Set-up for measuring swelling pressure in the constant volume method**

4. Place the load measuring proving ring tip attached to the load frame in contact with the consolidation cell without any eccentricity.
5. Fit a strain measuring dial gauge to the cell.
6. Inundate the specimen with distilled water and allowed to swell.

7. Note the initial reading of the proving ring (Table 24.1).
8. Measure the swelling of the specimen with the help of dial gauge.
9. Adjust the platen such that the dial gauge (deformation zero) always show the original reading. This adjustment shall be done at every 0.1 mm of swell or earlier.
10. Test should be continued till no more (or negligible) swelling (increase in volume) takes place.
11. The assembly extracted from the consolidation ring to determine final moisture content.

TABLE 24.1

Swelling pressure test by constant volume method

Project: Dated: Tested by:

Details of soil sample

(*i*) Location

(*ii*) Bore hole No. Depth

(*iii*) Visual description of soil

(*iv*) Liquid limit: Plasticity index

(*v*) Percentage of soil fraction below 0.002 mm

Details of soil specimen

(*i*) Undisturbed or remoulded

(*ii*) Specific gravity of the soil

(*iii*) Moisture content (%)

(*iv*) Dry density (g/cc)

Date	Time	Dial gauge reading before adjustment	Proving-ring Reading	Load in kg	Swell pressure in kg/cm^2	Remarks

CALCULATIONS AND REPORT

The difference between the final and initial dial readings of the proving ring gives total load in terms of division which when multiplied by calibration factor gives the total load. This when divided by the cross-sectional area of the soil specimen gives the swelling pressure expressed in kg/cm^2 (or in kPa).

Swelling pressure in kg/cm^2 (or in kPa) = $(P_f - P_i) \times CF/A$

where

P_f = Final reading of proving ring

P_i = Initial reading of proving ring

CF = Calibration factor of the proving ring

A = Area of the specimen ($\pi d^2/4$)

d = diameter of the specimen

The free swell index is expressed as a percentage to two significant figures.

25

DETERMINATION OF FREE SWELL INDEX OF SOIL

AIM

To determine the free swell index of a given soil.

THEORY AND APPLICATION

Swelling and shrinking of soil leads to distress in the substructure resulting in failure of foundation. Swelling of soils exerts upward pressure on the foundation. The amount of pressure exerted by the soil depends on the amount of increase in volume. In Chapters 23 and 24 the procedure to measure the swelling pressure in soils is explained. The swelling pressure test provide the actual pressure that the soil could exert on foundation which can directly incorporated in design calculations. However, the procedure to estimate the swelling pressure is time consuming and it needs specialized equipment. To identify a soil as expansive a quick test is designed which is based on the measurement of volume change of soil when it comes in contact with water. The increase in volume as a percentage of initial volume of soil is referred as free swell index of soil.

APPARATUS AND MATERIAL

1. Graduated glass cylinders of 100 cc capacity - 2 Nos.
2. A sieve (425 μ).

3. Sensitive balance (accuracy 0.01g)
4. Kerosene

PROCEDURE

1. Take 10 g of oven dry soil sample passing through 425 μ sieve and pour into a 100 cc graduated jar. Similarly, prepare another cylinder with same weight of soil.
2. Fill one jar with kerosene oil and the other with distilled water up to the 100 cc mark.
3. Remove the entrapped air from both the cylinders by shaking and/or stirring with a glass rod.
4. Allow both the cylinders to settle down for 24 hours.
5. Read out the level of the soil in the kerosene-filled graduated jar (V_k). Kerosene being non-polar liquid, does not cause swelling of soil.
6. Read the level of soil in the distilled water-filled graduated jar (V_d).

CALCULATIONS

The free swell index of the soil is computed using Eq. (25.1)

$$\text{Free swell index} = (V_d - V_k) / V_k \times 100 \qquad (25.1)$$

where

V_d = volume of soil in distilled water after 24 hours

V_k = volume of soil in kerosene oil after 24 hours

RESULTS

The free swell index is expressed as a percentage to two significant figures.

26

STANDARD PENETRATION TEST (SPT)

AIM

To perform standard penetration test to obtain the penetration resistance (N-value) along the depth at a given site.

THEORY AND APPLICATION

The standard penetration test (SPT) is a standardized method of sounding (IS: 2131; ASTM D1586). The test is performed at the site in a clean bore-hole of 55 mm to 150 mm diameter. A casing or drilling mud is used to support the sides of the bore hole if required.

In this test, a thick wall standard split spoon sampler, 50.8 mm outer diameter and 35 mm inner diameter, is driven into the undisturbed soil at the bottom of the bore hole under the blows of a 63.5 kg drive weight with 75 cm free fall. The minimum open length of the sampler should be 60 cm. The number of blows required to drive the sampler 30 cm beyond the seating drive of 15 cm, is termed as the penetration resistance N. There are a number of empirical relationships available between N-values and relative density, unit weight, angle of internal friction ϕ, bearing capacity of soils as shown in Tables 26.1 and 26.2.

From Tables 26.1 and 26.2 it can be observed that by obtaining the N-value at a location, the soil properties can be approximately assessed. Knowing the angle of internal friction ϕ, of gravelly soils the bearing capacity factors N_q and N_γ can be read from standard Tables or charts and the bearing capacity of foundation can be estimated.

TABLE 26.1

Empirical values of γ, D_r and φ of cohesionless soils based on the corrected N-value (Bowles, 1982)

N-Value	Nature of soil	Relative density, D_r (%)	Unit weight, γ (T/m^3)	Approximate angle of internal friction, φ°
5 - 6	Very loose – Losse	15	1.1 - 1.8	27 - 32°
8 - 15	Loose – Medium	35	1.4 - 2.0	30 - 35°
10 - 40	Medium – Dense	65	1.7 - 2.2	35 - 40°
20 - 70	Dense – Very dense	85	1.7 - 2.3	38 - 43°
> 35	Very dense	100	2.0 - 2.3	-

TABLE 26.2

Empirical values of unconfined compressive strength of clay soils based on N - value

N-Value	Nature of soil	Unconfined compressive strength, q_u (kPa)
2	Very soft – Soft	25
4	Soft – Medium	50
8	Medium – Stiff	100
16	Stiff – Very stiff	200
32	Very stiff – Hard	400

Further, Terzaghi and Peck (1948) proposed correlation in the form of curves for estimating the allowable soil pressure (q_{na}) for footings resting on sand (for a limiting settlement of 25 mm). Teng (1962) provided the Eq. (26.1), which closely approximates the curves presented by Terzaghi and Peck (1948).

$$q_{na} = 34.5\,(N - 3)\,(0.305\,B + 1)/(0.7B) \quad (26.1)$$

where q_{na} = net allowable soil pressure for a permissible settlement of 25 mm in (kN/m^2).

B = width of footing in metres

Similarly Meyerhof (1956) suggested a correlation as given in Eqs. (26.2) and (26.3)

$$q_{na} = 12\,N \qquad \text{for } B \leq 1.22 \text{ m} \quad (26.2)$$

$$q_{na} = 8N\,(0.305\,B + 1)/(0.305B) \qquad \text{for } B > 1.22 \text{ m} \quad (26.3)$$

where q_{na} and B having the same meaning and units as in Eq. (26.1).

The Eqs. (26.1), (26.2) and (26.3) are for a limiting settlement of 25 mm.

However, the allowable soil pressure (q'_{na}) for any settlement (S′) is given by

$$q'_{na} = (q_{na})\, S'/25 \qquad (26.4)$$

where q'_{na} is the net allowable soil pressure (in Kpa) corresponding to the settlement S′ (in mm). The correlations represented in Eqs. (26.1) to (26.4) are applicable to situations in which the water table is at least 2B below the foundation level where B is the width of footing. The N-value represented is the corrected values. If the water table is at or close to the foundation level the allowable soil pressure has to be reduced by 50% for the same permissible settlement.

APPARATUS

1. Tripod (to give a clear height of about 4 m; one of the legs of the tripod should have ladder to facilitate a person to reach tripod head).
2. Tripod head with hook.
3. Pulley.
4. Guide pipe assembly (with a 75 cm clear travel for the standard 63.5 kg weight and provision to connect to A-drill extension rods).
5. Standard split spoon sampler.
6. A-dril rods (heavy duty) for extending the test to deeper depths; number of rods depends on the depth of exploration.
7. Heavy duty Post hole auger (100 mm or 150 mm diameter) .

8. Heavy duty helical auger.
9. Heavy duty auger extension rods (Number of rods depends on the depth of exploration)
10. Sand bailer.
11. Manular rope (about 15 m long strong enough to lift 63.5 kg load repeatedly).
12. A light duty rope to operate sand bailer.
13. Chain pulley block (to pull out casing pipes etc).
14. Casing pipes (100 mm diameter or 150 mm diameter depending on the diameter of the auger in use). Number of casing pipes depends on the depth of exploration.
15. Casing couplings
16. Casing clamps
17. Measuring tape
18. A straight edge (50 cm long)
19. Toolbox with spanner set, chain winches, pipe winches, screw drivers etc.
20. Piece of chalk (or any other marker).
21. Other general materials such as oil can, cotton waste, wire clamps, crowbar, spade etc.
22. If a machine is employed to apply the blows a minimum of 6 labors are required to shift the tripod from place to place and to advance auger manually. If the blows are to be given by manual operation then a total of 10 laborers are required for this testing programme.

PROCEDURE

The testing procedure is explained in the following steps

1. Identify the location of testing in the field.
2. Erect the tripod such that the top of the tripod head is centrally located over the testing spot. This can be reasonably ensured by passing a rope over the pulley connected to the tripod head and making the free end of the rope to come down and adjusting the tripod legs such that the rope end is at the

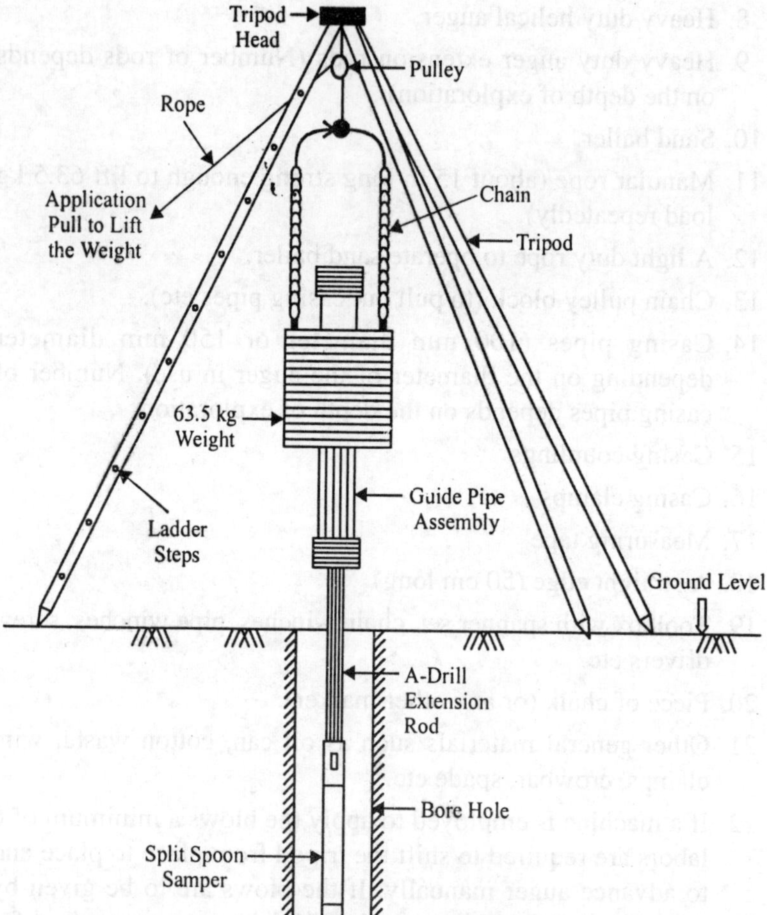

Figure 26.1 **: Line sketch of SPT Set-up**

testing spot. While erecting and adjusting the tripod legs, care should be taken to see that the load is uniformly distributed over the three legs. This can be achieved by ensuring the lines joining the tips of the tripod legs on the ground forms an equilateral triangle. Further, it should be ensured that the three legs of the tripod are firmly supported on the ground (i.e. the soil below the legs should not be loose and they should not be supported on a sloping rock surface or on a small boulder which may tilt during testing).

3. Advance the bore-hole, at the test location, using the auger. To start with advance the bore-hole for a depth of 0.5 m and clear the loose soil from the bore hole.
4. Clean the split spoon sampler and apply a thin film of oil to the inside face of the sampler. Connect an A-drill extension rod to the split spoon sampler.
5. Slip the 63.6 kg weight on to the guide pipe assembly and connect the guide pipe assembly to the other end of the A-drill rod.
6. The chain connected to the driving weight (63.5 kg) is tied to the Manila rope passing over the pulley at the tripod head as shown in Fig. 26.1. The other end of the rope is pulled down manually or with help of mechanical winch. By pulling the rope down, the drive weight, guide pipe assembly, A-drill rod and the split spoon sampler will get vertically erected.
7. A person should hold the guide pipe assembly split spoon sampler to be vertical with the falling weight lowered to the bottom of the guide pipe assembly.
8. Now place a straight edge across the bore touching the A-drill rod. Mark the straight edge level (i.e. approximately the ground level) all round the A-drill rod with the help of a chalk or any other marker. From this mark, measure up along the A-drill rod and mark 15 cm, 30 cm and 45 cm above the straight edge level.
9. Lift the driving weight to reach the top of the guide pipe assembly travel and allow it to fall freely. The fall of driving weight will transfer the impact load to the split spoon sampler, which drive the split spoon sampler into the ground. Again lift the drive weight to the top of travel and allow it to fall freely under its own weight from a height of 75-cm (clear travel in the guide pipe assembly) is called as a blow. As the number of blows are applied, the split spoon sampler will penetrate into the ground and the first mark (15 cm mark) on the drill rod approaches the straight edge (i.e. ground level).

10. Count the number of blows required for the first 15 cm, second 15 cm and the third 15 cm mark to cross down the straight edge.
11. The penetration of the first 15 cm is considered as the seating drive and the number of blows required for this penetration is noted but not accounted in computing penetration resistance value. The total number of blows required for the penetration of the split spoon sampler by 2nd and 3rd 15 cm is recorded as the penetration resistance or N-value.
12. After the completion of the split spoon sampler by 45 cm, pull out the whole assembly (split spoon sampler, A-drill rod and guide pipe assembly with weight). Detach the split sampler from A-drill rod and open it out. Collect the soil sample from the split spoon sampler into a sampling bag. Store the sampling bag safely with an identification tag for laboratory investigation.
13. Advance the bore hole by another 1m (i.e. depth of penetration of the sampler, 45 cm + 55 cm) or till a change of soil strata which ever is early.
14. Clean the split spoon sampler, apply a thin film of oil and connect it to guide pipe assembly (if require add an additional A-drill rod). Repeat the test.
15. The test is repeated with advancement of bore hole till the required depth of exploration is reached or till a refusal condition is encountered. (Refusal condition is said to exist if the number of blows required for the last 30 cm of penetration is more than 100). The depth of exploration depends on the required bearing capacity, depth of foundation and width of foundation. Generally the depth of exploration twice the width of foundation below the foundation level.
16. The test will be repeated in number of bore holes covering the site depending on the building area, importance of the structure and the variation of the soil properties across the site.
17. The SPT observations are presented either in the form of Table 26.3 or in the form of bore log data as shown in Fig. 26.2

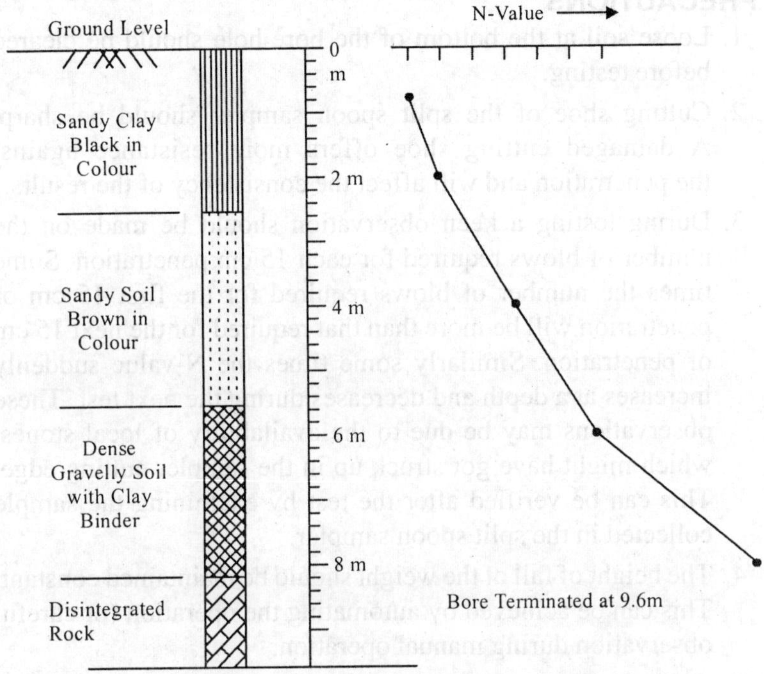

Figure 26.2 **: Typical representation SPT results in a bore-log**

TABLE 26.3

Standard penetration test (SPT) observations

Project : Site location :

General soil condition :

Depth of water table below ground level :

Borehole Identification No.	Depth of testing (m)	N - value	Remarks

PRECAUTIONS

1. Loose soil at the bottom of the bore hole should be cleared before testing.
2. Cutting shoe of the split spoon sampler should be sharp. A damaged cutting shoe offers more resistance against the penetration and will affect the consistency of the results.
3. During testing a keen observation should be made on the number of blows required for each 15 cm penetration. Some times the number of blows required for the first 15 cm of penetration will be more than that required for the next 15 cm of penetration. Similarly some times the N-value suddenly increases at a depth and decreases during the next test. These observations may be due to the availability of local stones, which might have got struck up in the sampler cutting edge. This can be verified after the test by examining the sample collected in the split spoon sampler.
4. The height of fall of the weight should be maintained constant. This can be achieved by automating the operation (or careful observation during manual operation.
5. Guide pipe assembly should be maintained perfect vertical so that no significant friction is developed between the falling weight and the guide pipe assembly.

Correction to N-value

The N-value observed during testing is not utilised directly in assessing the soil properties. These values are corrected to account for

1. The overburden pressure
2. Dilatancy in saturated fine sands and silts.

Correction for over burden pressure

The penetration resistance of soil depends on the over burden pressure. At deeper depth in-situ soil will have higher overburden pressure hence its response to SPT test will be better when compared to the behavior of the same soil at shallow depth.

Bazaraa (1967 Bowles, p99) proposed the following corrections to the actual count N, based on the over burden pressure

For $p_0 \leq 75$ kPa $\quad N' = 4N/(1+0.04p_0)$ ...(26.5)

For p0 > 75 kPa $\quad N' = 4N/(3.25 + 0.01p_0)$ ...(26.6)

where

N' = corrected N-value

N = observed N-value

p_0 = over burden pressure, (kPa) (γD)

D = depth of testing (m)

γ = unit weight of soil at the time of testing (kN/m^3)

From Eqs. (26.5) and (26.6) it may be observed that

1. N′ is increased from the actual blow count when $p_0 \leq 75$ kPa.
2. N′ is decreased from the actual blow count when $p_0 > 75$ kPa.

Correction for the dilatancy in saturated fine sands and silts

When dynamic loads are applied on silty and fine sandy soils in saturated state the pore pressure in such soils will not be in a position to get dissipated due to low permeability. Hence, during dynamic loading (i.e. application of blows) the pore water will offer a temporary resistance to dynamic loads. This leads to higher value of N-value which is unsafe. Therefore when SPT is performed in saturated silts and fine sands and if the observed N-value is more than 15 a correction has to be applied to reduce the observed values. This correction is applied on the N-value corrected for over burden pressure (N′).

If the stratum (during testing) consists of fine sand and silt below water table, the corrected N-value (N′) has to be further corrected to get the final corrected value N″

$$N'' = 15 + \tfrac{1}{2}(N' - 15)$$

RESULTS

1. N-value at different depth
2. Type of soil with depth.

27

PLATE LOAD TEST (PLT)

AIM

To perform plate load test to obtain a load-settlement curve of a soil at a particular depth so as to estimate the ultimate bearing capacity, allowable soil pressure for a limiting foundation settlement.

THEORY AND APPLICATION

Plate load test is a field test to determine the ultimate bearing capacity of soil, and the probable settlement under a given loading. This test is covered in IS: 1888 and ASTM D1194. The test essentially consists of loading a rigid plate at the foundation level, and determining the settlement corresponding to each load increment. The ultimate bearing capacity is then taken as the load at which the plate start sinking at a rapid rate. The method assumes that down to the depth of influence of stresses, the soil strata is reasonably uniform.

The bearing plate is either square or circular, of minimum recommended size 300 mm and maximum of 750 mm. The plate should have a thickness sufficient to withstand bending stresses that would be caused by the maximum anticipated load. The thickness of steel plate should not be less than 25 mm. The small size (300 mm) plate is adopted for dense soils and large plates are used for tests in soft or weak soils. This is because for an applied load the stress intensity transferred on to the ground is inversely proportional to the size of the plate. Hence, by adopting large plate for soft soils small increments of stresses can be affected. Similarly for very dense soils by taking smaller plate, the ultimate bearing capacity of the soil can be achieved with a reasonable amount of reaction load.

Plate load test is mostly a confirmatory test. In order to perform this test, depth of foundation and possible safe bearing capacity or ultimate bearing stress of the soil should be known either from SPT or laboratory test. Plate load test will confirm the other test results and provides more information on the settlement behavior of foundation.

APPARATUS

1. Test plate (300 mm or 450 mm or 600 mm or 750 mm).
2. Hydraulic jack (50 T capacity).
3. Hydraulic pump (50 T capacity).
4. Pressure gauge (to read 50 T load with a sensitivity of 0.5T).
5. Proving ring or load cell (50 T capacity).
6. 4 dial gauges (with sensitivity of 0.01 mm and a travel of 50 mm).
7. Loading columns.
8. Dial gauge supporting channels.
9. Dial gauge stands.
10. Magnetic bases for dial gauges.
11. Loading platform equipment (Girders, plates, sand bags etc) or Truss with anchor rods.
12. Plumb
13. Spirit level
14. Tripod (to erect the platform or truss frame).
15. Pulley block (to lift the girders or truss frame).
16. Toolbox with spanner set, etc.
17. Crowbar

PROCEDURE

1. Excavate the test pit. The test pit size should be 5 times the size of test plate (B_p) and the depth equal to the depth of foundation.

2. The loading platform (two types of loading platforms commonly in use are shown in Fig. 27.1 and 27.2) should be erected over the test pit such that, the vertical line drawn through the center of gravity (CG) of the load passes through the centroid of the base of the test pit. This can be achieved by positioning the reaction girder (truss) with the help of the plum bob and spirit level. The load over the platform should be at least 50% more than the anticipated load to be transferred on to the plate. This will ensure the safety of the platform for any small shift of the CG of the loading platform from the vertical axis of the pit.
3. Position the test plate centrally at the base of the pit. Ensure that the ground surface below the test plate is perfectly horizontal and level so that no stress concentration takes place below the plate during loading. If the ground surface is slightly uneven a thin layer of sand is spread underneath the test plate.
4. Position the hydraulic jack over the plate so that when hydraulic pressure is built up the jack pushes against the loading platform. If require place a loading column between the test plate and the jack so as to ensure the jack reach the loading platform (or truss) as shown in Fig. 27.1 (or Fig. 27.2).
5. Position a minimum of two dial gauges diagonally at the corners (preferably 4 at all corners of the test plate) to record its settlement of the plate. The dial gauges should be supported carefully over a stable base which do not settle with the plate. This can be achieved by placing two cross beams at ground level over which the dial gauges are supported with the help of magnetic bases as shown in Fig. 27.1. The settlement of the plate is transmitted to the dial gauges through dial gauge stands as shown in Fig. 27.1.
6. The dial gauges should be positioned such that the plunger of the dial gauge is at its beginning of rebound (i.e. the plunger is initially pushed up) so that it will get released as the plate settles and the reading changes (decreases) and the difference in reading provides the settlement of the plate.

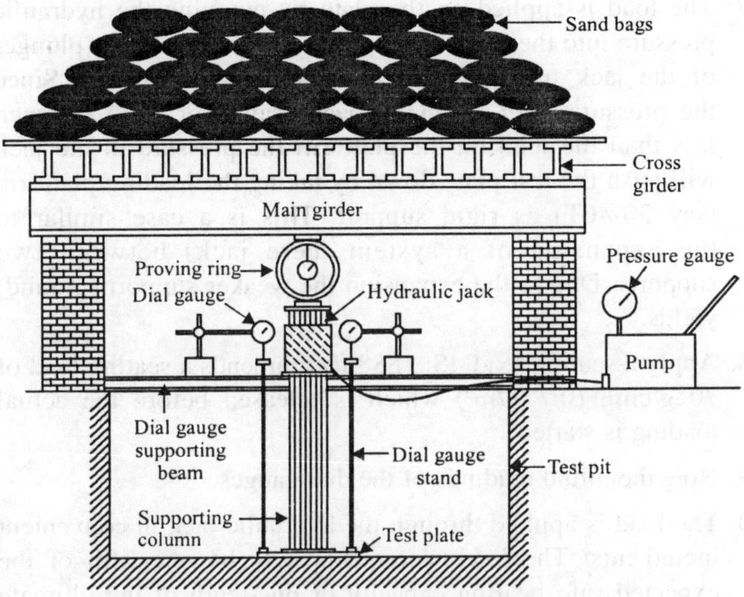

***Figure 27.1* : Reaction loading platform**

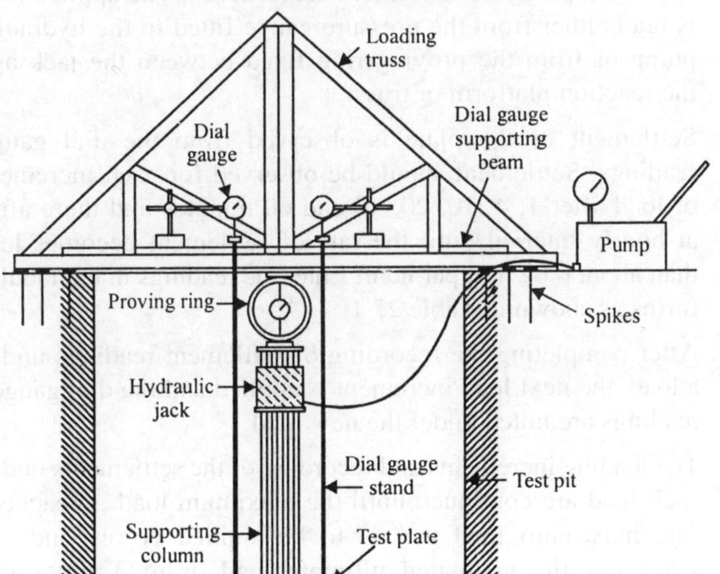

***Figure 27.2* : Loading truss**

7. The load is applied on the plate by pumping the hydraulic pressure into the jack. The upward movement of the plunger of the jack tries to push the loading platform up. Since the pressure built up in the jack (say 1 or 2 T) is much less than the load on the platform the pressure in the jack will push the test plate down by taking the loading platform (say 30-40T) as rigid support. This is a case similar to the expansion of a system (here jack) between two supports. Due to the expansion the weaker support (ground) yields.
8. Apply a seating load. IS: 1888 recommends a seating load of 70 g/cm^2, (0.7 T/m^2) which is released before the actual loading is started.
9. Note the initial readings of the dial gauges.
10. The load is applied through the hydraulic jack in convenient increments. The load increments may be one fifth of the expected safe bearing capacity or one-tenth of the ultimate bearing capacity or any other smaller loads. The applied load is read either from the pressure gauge fitted to the hydraulic pump or from the proving ring fixed between the jack and the reaction platform or truss.
11. Settlement of the plate is observed from the dial gauge readings. Settlement should be observed for each increment of load after 1; 4, 10, 20, 40 and 60 minutes and there after at hourly interval until the rate of settlement becomes less than about 0.02 mm per hour. Enter the readings in the tabular forms as shown in Table 27.1.
12. After completing the recording of settlement readings under a load, the next load increment is applied and the dial gauges readings are noted under the new load.
13. The loading increments and recording of the settlements under each load are continued until the maximum load is reached. The maximum load that is to be applied corresponds to 1.5 times the estimated ultimate load or to 3 times the proposed allowable bearings pressure.

Precautions and Limitations of the Plate load test

1. The water table has a marked influence on the bearing capacity of sandy or gravelly soil. If the water table is already above the level of the footing, it should be lowered by pumping and the bearing plate seated after the water table has been lowered just below the footing level. Even if the water table is located less than 1 m below the base level of the footing the load test should be made at the level of the water table itself. This is because, if the water table is less than 1m below the base of the footing (test plate) the soil between the test plate and the water table will be filled with capillary water. The capillary zone of soil show a higher stiffness. This results in the over estimation of bearing capacity, which is unsafe.
2. The test results reflect only the characteristics of the soil located within a depth less than twice the width of the bearing plate (corresponding to an isobar of one-tenth the loading intensity at the test plate). Since the foundations are generally larger, the settlement and the resistance against shear failure depend on the properties of a much thicker stratum.
3. It is essentially short duration test, and hence the test does not give the ultimate settlement, particularly in the case of cohesive soils.
4. In dense sandy soils, the bearing capacity increases with the size of the foundation, and the tests on smaller size bearing plate tend to give conservative values.

OBSERVATIONS AND CALCULATIONS

The load intensity and settlement observations of the plate load test (from Table 27.1) are plotted. Fig. 27.3 shows a set of typical load settlement curves. The ultimate bearing capacity is taken as the load at which the plate start sinking at a rapid rate, i.e. when the curve drops down to a vertical line. From Fig. 27.3 it can be observed that in dense sands or stiff clays the failure is well defined; where as in loose sands or soft clays the failure is not pronounced. In such cases a plot of load and settlement, both

TABLE 27.1

Plate load test observations (Sheet No. 1)

Project   Site location :   Depth of Testing :   Depth of water table :   Date :

Load (kN)	Time	Settlement Dial gaugue-I			Settlement Dial gaugue-2			Settlement Dial gauge-3			Settlement Dial guage-4			Average Settle-ment
		Dial gauge reading	Settle-ment (mm)	Cumul-ative settle-ment (mm)	Dial gauge reading	Settle-ment (mm)	Cumul-ative settle-ment (mm)	Dial gauge reading	Settle-ment (mm)	Cumul-ative settle-ment (mm)	Dial gauge reading	Settle-ment (mm)	Cumul-ative settle-ment (mm)	

TABLE 27.2

Plate load test observations (Sheet No. 2)

Project Site location : Depth of Testing : Depth of water table : Date :

Load (kN)	Time	Settlement Dial gaugue-I			Settlement Dial gaugue-2			Settlement Dial gauge-3			Settlement Dial guage-4			Average Settle-ment
		Dial gauge reading	Settle-ment (mm)	Cumul-ative settle-ment (mm)	Dial gauge reading	Settle-ment (mm)	Cumul-ative settle-ment (mm)	Dial gauge reading	Settle-ment (mm)	Cumul-ative settle-ment (mm)	Dial gauge reading	Settle-ment (mm)	Cumul-ative settle-ment (mm)	

TABLE 27.3

Plate load test observations (Sheet No. 3)

Project Site location : Depth of Testing : Depth of water table : Date :

Load (kN)	Time	Settlement Dial gaugue-I			Settlement Dial gaugue-2			Settlement Dial gauge-3			Settlement Dial guage-4			Average Settle-ment
		Dial gauge reading	Settle-ment (mm)	Cumul-ative settle-ment (mm)	Dial gauge reading	Settle-ment (mm)	Cumul-ative settle-ment (mm)	Dial gauge reading	Settle-ment (mm)	Cumul-ative settle-ment (mm)	Dial gauge reading	Settle-ment (mm)	Cumul-ative settle-ment (mm)	

TABLE 27.4

Plate load test observations (Sheet No. 4)

Project Site location : Depth of Testing : Depth of water table : Date :

Load (kN)	Time	Settlement Dial gaugue-I			Settlement Dial gaugue-2			Settlement Dial gauge-3			Settlement Dial guage-4			Average Settlement
		Dial gauge reading	Settlement (mm)	Cumulative settlement (mm)	Dial gauge reading	Settlement (mm)	Cumulative settlement (mm)	Dial gauge reading	Settlement (mm)	Cumulative settlement (mm)	Dial gauge reading	Settlement (mm)	Cumulative settlement (mm)	

being taken in logarithmic scales, gives two straight lines. The intersection of these lines is taken as the ultimate bearing capacity of soil (see Fig. 27.4).

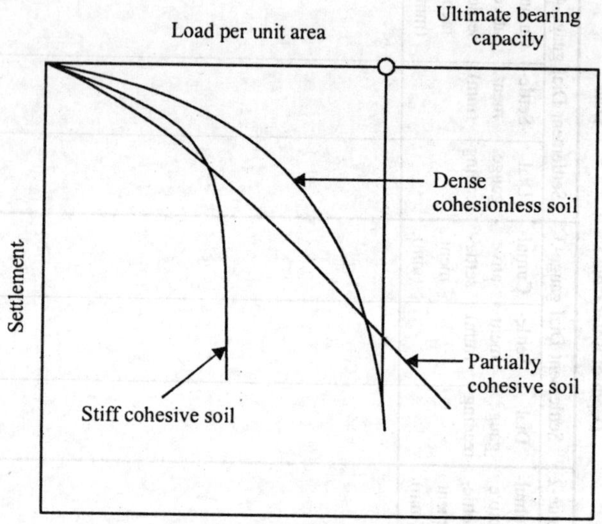

Figure 27.3 **: Typical load settlement curves**

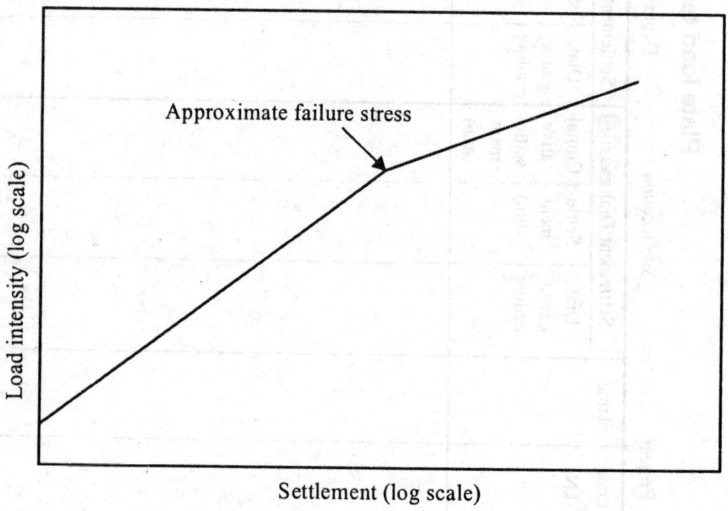

Figure 27.4 **: Plate load test curve on log-lot scale**

The safe bearing capacity is calculated from the ultimate bearing capacity allowing a certain factor of safety (a factor of safety of 2-3 is recommended depending on the uniformity of the soil at the site and the test conditions). In case of sandy soils, the plate settlement (S_p) corresponding to the safe soil pressure from the graph is found. The footing settlement (S_f) is computed from Eq. (27.1). If the settlement (S_f) is less than the permissible settlement, then the safe bearing pressure computed above is the allowable soil pressure. Otherwise S_f is made equal to permissible settlement and the plate settlement S_p is computed back from Eq. (27.1). Then the soil pressure corresponding to this S_p in the load-settlement curve is the allowable soil pressure.

$$S_f = S_p \ \{B_f (B_p + 0.3)\}/\{B_p (B_f + 0.3)\}]^2 \qquad ...(27.1)$$

where S_f = settlement of footing (mm)

S_p = settlement of plate (mm)

B_f = width of footing (m)

B_p = width of plate (m)

The plate load test is adequate for light or less important structures under normal conditions. However, in the case of unusual soil types and for all heavy and special structures the plate load test results have to be supplemented with additional laboratory tests. In order to arrive at a reasonable value for settlement and allowable bearing capacity, tests at different depths and with different sizes of plate have to be done. This is expensive and time consuming. However, plate load test is best suited in weak jointed rocks or soils containing large gravel or boulders.

RESULTS

Allowable bearing capacity of soil =

Settlement of footing at the allowable bearing capacity =

28

FIELD DETERMINATION OF CALIFORNIA BEARING RATIO (CBR)

AIM

To determine California bearing ratio (CBR) of soil in-place for the evaluation of strength of sub-grade and bases for roads and runway pavements.

THEORY AND APPLICATIONS

California bearing ratio (CBR) is defined as the ratio of the force required to penetrate a soil mass with a standard circular piston at the rate of 1.25 mm/min. to that required for corresponding penetration into a standard material (crushed stone) which has a bearing ratio of 100%.

California bearing ratio is an adhoc penetration test used for the evaluation of strengths of sub-grade and bases for roads and runway pavements. The results obtained by these tests are used in conjunction with empirical curves, based on experience for the design of flexible pavement (Khanna and Jestoe.). The test gives empirical strength values which may not be directly related to fundamental properties governing the strength of soil.

The test is either performed in the laboratory on undisturbed or remoulded soil specimen or directly on the field. Where facilities for reaction loading are not available undisturbed samples may be obtained and tested in the laboratory. The laboratory test procedure is explained in Chapter Twenty.

APPARATUS

1. **Loading device:** A mechanical screw loading jack with swivel head for applying load to the penetration piston. The device should have an arrangement for attaching to truck, tractor, truss or any other equipment used to provide load reaction. The jack should be such that, a uniform penetration rate of 1.25 mm/min can be achieved. The minimum capacity of the jack should be 5000 kg.
2. **Equipment for providing reaction for loading:** Truck, tractor, truss or any other suitable equipment. If truck or tractor is used they should be loaded suitably to give the necessary reaction. If truss is used it should be suitably anchored.
3. **Jacks:** Two tracks-type jacks of 5 to 12 tonnes capacity and having double action combination trip and automatic lowering in cases where loaded truck or tractor is used for necessary reaction.
4. **Proving ring:** One calibrated proving ring of capacity 5000 kg with a dial gauge to read to an accuracy of 0.002 mm and having a travel of 5 mm. The proving ring should have an accuracy of 0.5% of the load measured.
5. **Metal penetration piston:** 50 ± 0.1 mm in diameter and not less than 100 mm long.
6. **Extensions:** Internally threaded pipe or rod extensions not less than 200 cm long furnished in the following quantities and lengths (the values in the table are only for guidance, any other convenient lengths may also be used).

Length of Extension (cm)	Number of Extensions
5	2
10	2
20	1
30	1
50	1
100	1

7. **Connectors:** For coupling the penetration piston and proving ring assembly either directly or through extension pieces.
8. **Dial gauge:** One dial gauge having a least count of 0.01 mm and a travel of 25 mm, for measuring the penetration of the piston.
9. **Dial gauge support:** Rigid and of steel angle welded connection or light alloy pipe construction about 2 m long, of overall height. 30 cm and 45 cm wide at the feet with universal or ordinary dial gauge holder adjustable anywhere along the length of the support.
10. **Surcharge weight:** One annular metal weight weighing 5 kg and of 250 mm diameter with a central hole 53 mm in diameter. The circular slotted weights of weight 5 kg and of diameter 215 to 250 mm with a central hole and slot width of 53 mm. Two circular slotted weights of weight 10 kg and of diameter 215 to 250 mm with a central hole and slot width of 53 mm.
11. **Miscellaneous Apparatus:** Other general apparatus, such as spirit level, pick, spade, scoop and brush, apparatus for moisture content and density determination.

PROCEDURE

1. If the surface to be tested is at a depth below ground level, excavate a test pit having a minimum dimensions of 0.5 m × 0.5 m to a depth where test is to be performed. The surface area to be tested should be exposed, cleaned of all loose and dried material and leveled. Since the test measures the soil at shallow depths, extreme care should be taken not to disturb the test surface.
2. If the actual service conditions in the field warrant, the surface to be tested may be soaked to the desired degree using surcharge weights, if necessary. The test surface should be drained of all free water and allowed to stand at least 15 minutes before starting further operations.
3. The equipment used to provide load reaction (truck, tractor, truss etc.), should be so located that the centre of the beam

against which the loading jack will work is over the centre of the surface to be tested.

4. The screw jack with swivel should be installed to the under side of the equipment providing reaction, at the correct position of the test.
5. Connect the proving ring to the bottom end of the jack and the piston connector to the bottom of the proving ring. (use the extension pipes if necessary)
6. Ensure that the entire assembly is plumb and the loading jack should be clamped in position.
7. Surcharge annular weight of 5 kg kept in position on the surface to be tested, so that when the piston is lowered it will pass through the hole in the annular weight.
8. The penetration piston should be seated with a small load (< 4 kg) so that full contact is established between the piston and the surface to be tested. For material with irregular surface the piston may be seated on a thin layer of plaster of paris spread over the surface.
9. While the seating load is on the piston, a 3 to 6 mm layer of clean sand should be spread over the surface to be covered by the surcharge annular weight. This helps in distributing the surcharge load over the surface uniformly.
10. Surcharge weights, sufficient to produce an intensity of loading equal to the weight of the base material and pavement, except that the minimum weight applied should be 15 kg including that of the annular weight.
11. The penetration indicating dial should be suitably fixed for reading the penetration and the dial set to zero. A diagrammatic set up of the test is shown in Fig. 28.1
12. Apply the load on the penetration piston so that the penetration is approximately 1.25 mm/min.
13. Record the load readings at penetrations of 0, 0.5, 1.0, 1.5, 2.0, 2.5, 3.0, 4.0, 5.0, 7.5, 10.0 and 12.5 mm. The maximum load (not exceeding proving ring capacity) and corresponding

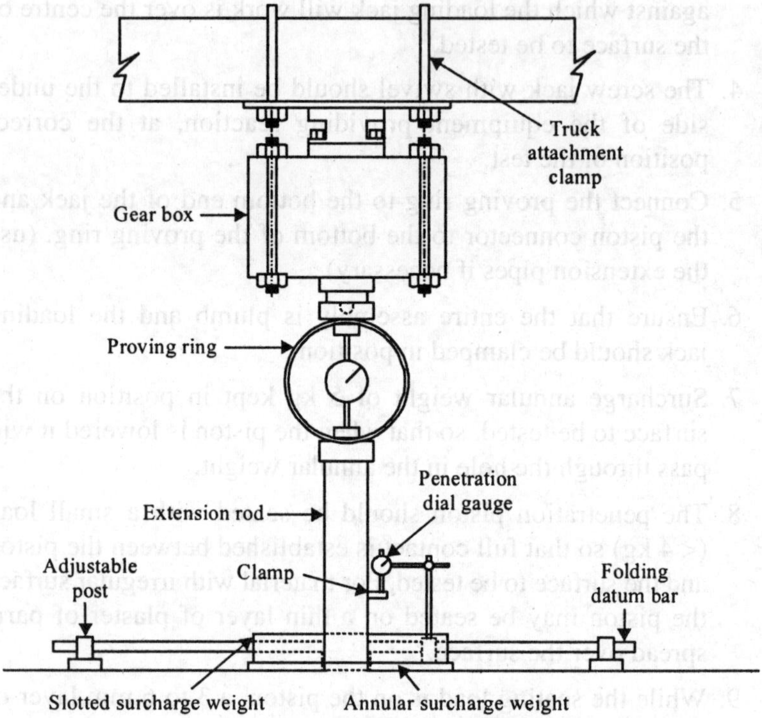

Figure 28.1 **: Field CBR Apparatus**

penetration is recorded if it occurs for a penetration less than 12.5 mm. The observations should be recorded in Table 28.1

14. Dismantle the set up.
15. After completing the test, collect a soil sample at the point of penetration, for moisture content determination.

OBSERVATIONS AND CALCULATIONS

The load and penetration readings should be recorded in Table 28.1. Using the data, plot the load penetration curve. This curve will be mainly convex upwards although the initial portion of the curve may be, some times, concave upwards due to surface irregularities. A correction shall than be applied by drawing a tangent to the curve at the point of greatest slope (as explained in Chapter Twenty). The corrected curve shall be taken to be this tangent together with the convex portion of the original curve with the origin of strains shifted to the point where the tangent cuts the horizontal strain axis as illustrated in Fig. 20.2

Computation of CBR

Corresponding to the penetration value at which the bearing ratio is desired, correct load values shall be taken from the load penetration curve and the bearing ratio calculated as follows:

$$\text{California Bearing Ratio} = P_T/P_s \times 100$$

where

P_T = corrected load corresponding to the chosen penetration value read from the load penetration curve, in kg; and

P_S = Standard load for the same depth of penetration as per P_T taken from Table 28.2 in kg.

TABLE 28.1
Observations for field CBR Test

Project : Location : Tested by :

Depth of test point : Date :

Condition of test surface : soaked/unsoaked

Period of soaking if any : Surcharge weight during soaking :

Moisture content : Density:

Surcharge weight used during testing :

Penetration Dial gauge	Penetration (mm)	Proving ring reading	Load (kg)	Corrected load (kg)
	0.5			
	1.0			
	1.5			
	2.0			
	2.5			
	3.0			
	4.0			
	5.0			
	7.5			
	10.0			
	12.5			

TABLE 28.2
Standard loads for CBR Test

Penetration depth (mm)	Standard load (kg)
2.5	1370
5.0	2055
7.5	2630
10.0	3180
12.5	3600

RESULTS

CBR at 2.5 mm penetration =

CBR at 5 mm penetration =

Recommended CBR=

29

CYCLIC PLATE LOAD TEST

AIM

To determine the coefficient of elastic uniform compression (C_u) of soil by conducting cyclic plate load test.

THEORY AND APPLICATION

Coefficient of elastic uniform compression is a dynamic property of soil used in the design of machine foundation and other dynamic analysis of foundations. Coefficient of elastic uniform compression (C_u) is the compressive stress causing unit elastic compression for a given area under dynamic loading conditions.

The various parameters influencing the design of a machine foundation are: (*a*) centre of gravity, (*b*) moment of inertia of the base, (*c*) mass moment of inertia, (*d*) effective stiffness of the base support, and (*e*) damping. While parameters mentioned in (*a*), (*b*), (*c*) above may be called geometrical properties of the machine foundation system, the parameters (*d*) and (*e*) may be termed as physical properties of the elastic base of the foundation.

There are principally two schools of thought based on which the effective stiffness of soil under a machine foundation can be evaluated.

(*i*) Elastic half space theory

(*ii*) Linear spring analogy of soil

The elastic half space theory requires the determination of shear modulus (G) and the Poisson's ratio (ε) of soil preferably by an in situ dynamic test. The expression relating G and ε with the spring stiffness for a rigid circular footing resting on elastic half-space for different modes of vibration are as follows:

Vertical	$K_z = 4Gr_o/(1 - \varepsilon)$
Horizontal	$K_\tau = 32\,(1 - \varepsilon)\,Gr_o/(7.8\varepsilon)$
Rocking	$K_\theta = 8\,Gr_\theta^{\,3}/\{3\,(1 - \varepsilon)\}$
Torsion	$K_\psi = 16/3\,Gr_\psi^{\,3}$

where

$r_o = (A_f/\pi)^{0.5}$

$r_\theta = (4\,I_o/\pi)^{0.25}$

$r_\psi = (2I_z/\pi)^{9.25}$ where $I_z = I_x + I_y$

Similar expressions are available for rectangular footings (Srinivasulu and Vaidyanathan, 1977).

The theory based on the undamped linear spring analogy for soil, requires the evaluation of certain properties which are listed below:

(*i*) Coefficient of elastic uniform compression (C_u)

(*ii*) Coefficient of elastic uniform shear (C_τ)

(*iii*) Coefficient of elastic non-uniform compression (C_f)

(*iv*) Coefficient of elastic non-uniform shear (C_y)

The soil parameters mentioned above are used for the evaluation of the spring stiffness (K) of soil in various modes of vibration as presented below:

(*i*) For vertical motion $K_z = C_u A_f$

(*ii*) For horizontal (or sliding) motion $K_t = C_t A_f$

(*iii*) For rocking motion $K_q = C_q I_{x\,(\text{or}\,y)}$

(*iv*) For torsional motion (rotation about vertical axis) $K_y = C_y I_z$

where A_f is area of horizontal surface between foundation and soil, I is second moment of contact area about the horizontal axis (x or y) passing through the centroid of the base and normal to the plane of rocking, and I_z is second moment of inertia about the vertical axis passing through the centroid of the base.

The coefficient of elastic uniform compression (C_u) is defined as the ratio of compressive stress applied to a rigid foundation block to the elastic part of the settlement induced consequently. It has been reported that within a certain range of loading, there is a proportional relationship between the elastic settlement and the external uniform pressure on soil, the constant of proportionality being designated as the coefficient of elastic uniform compression (C_u). C_u is obtained by conducting either a cyclic plate load test or a block vibration test (under vertical vibrations).

This chapter explains the testing procedure and method of computing C_u from a cyclic plate load test.

APPARATUS

The equipment required to perform a plate load test as explained in Chapter Twenty seven are sufficient to conduct a cyclic plate load test.

PROCEDURE

1. Erect the platform and arrange the test plate, loading jack etc. as explained in Chapter 27.
2. After the set-up has been arranged note the initial readings of the dial gauges.
3. Apply the first increment of load on to the test plate.
4. Maintain the applied load constant throughout for a period till no further settlement occurs or the rate of settlement becomes negligible.
5. Record the final readings of the dial gauges.
6. Remove quickly but gradually the entire load and the plate is then allowed to rebound.

7. Again note the dial gauge readings when no further rebound occurs or the rate of rebound becomes negligible.
8. Increase the load gradually till its magnitude acquires a value equal to the proposed next higher stage of loading and maintain constant. Note the final reading of the dial gauges under the new load as explained earlier.
9. Reduce the entire load to zero and record the final dial gauge reading when the rate of rebound becomes negligible.
10. Continue the cycles of loading, unloading and reloading till the estimated ultimate load has been reached, the final values of dial gauge readings being noted each time.
11. The magnitude of the load increment should be such that the ultimate load is reached in five to six increments. The initial loading and unloading cycles up to the safe bearing capacity of the soil should be with smaller increments in load. The duration of each loading unloading cycle depends upon the type of soil under investigation. (Clay soils take more time and sandy soils take less time for each cycle).

OBSERVATIONS AND CALCULATIONS

The cyclic plate load test results are tabulated in the form of Table 29.1. (Table 29.1 is presented for the case where two dial gauges are used to measure the settlement. However, an extended table can be prepared when four dial gauges are used). Load settlement and rebound curve for the cyclic plate load test is plotted as shown in Fig. 29.1. From Fig. 29.1 obtain the elastic rebound (S_1, S_2, S_3, S_4) in soil under each applied load (P_1, P_2, P_3, P_4). Draw a graph between the loads (P_1, P_2, P_3, P_4) and the corresponding elastic rebound (S_1, S_2, S_3, S_4) value as shown in Fig. 29.2. The slope of the curve shown in Fig. 29.2 gives the value of coefficient of elastic uniform compression, C_u, which may be expressed as $C_u = P/S$ presented either in (kN/m^3) or in kg/cm^3

where

P = load intensity (kN/m^2) or (kg/cm^2) and

S = the corresponding elastic rebound (m) or (cm)

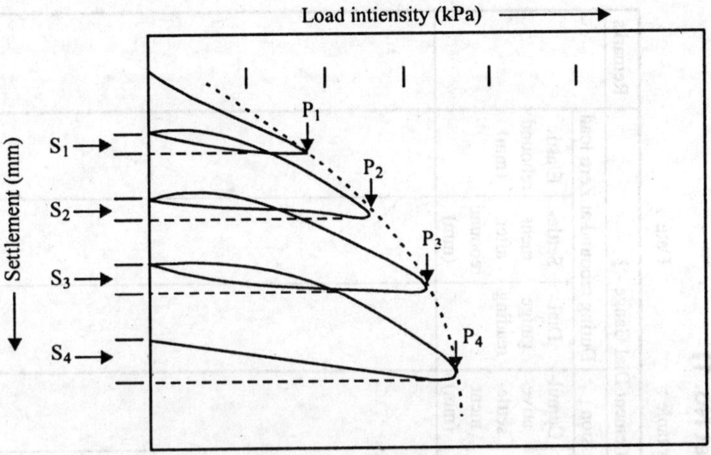

S_1, S_2, S_3, S_4 are elastic rebound at load P_1, P_2, P_3, P_4 respectively

Figure 29.1 **: Load settlement curve for cyclic plate load test**

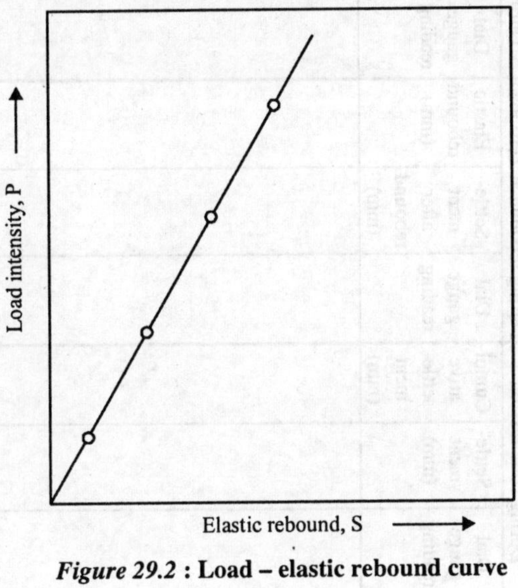

Figure 29.2 **: Load – elastic rebound curve**

RESULTS

Coefficient elastic uniform compression =

TABLE 29.1

Cyclic Plate load test observations (Sheet No. 1)

Project   Site location :   Depth of Testing :   Depth of water table :   Date :

Load (kN)	Time	Settlement Dial gaugue-I						Settlement Dial Gauge - 1						Remarks
		During compression			During rebound at Zero load			During compression			During rebound at Zero load			
		Dial gauge reading	Settlement (mm)	Cumulative settlement (mm)	Dial gauge reading	Settlement after rebound (mm)	Elastic rebound (mm)	Dial gauge reading	Settlement (mm)	Cumulative settlement (mm)	Dial gauge reading	Settlement after rebound (mm)	Elastic rebound (mm)	

TABLE 29.1

Cyclic Plate load test observations (Sheet No. 2)

Project

Site location : Depth of Testing : Depth of water table : Date :

Load (kN)	Time	Settlement Dial gaugue-I						Settlement Dial Gauge - 1						Remarks
		During compression			During rebound at Zero load			During compression			During rebound at Zero load			
		Dial gauge reading	Settle-ment (mm)	Cumul-ative settle-ment (mm)	Dial gauge reading	Settle-ment after rebound (mm)	Elastic rebound (mm)	Dial gauge reading	Settle-ment (mm)	Cumul-ative settle-ment (mm)	Dial gauge reading	Settle-ment after rebound (mm)	Elastic rebound (mm)	

TABLE 29.1

Cyclic Plate load test observations (Sheet No. 3)

Project   Site location :   Depth of Testing :   Depth of water table :   Date :

Load (kN)	Time	Settlement Dial gaugue-I						Settlement Dial Gauge - 1						Remarks
		During compression			During rebound at Zero load			During compression			During rebound at Zero load			
		Dial gauge reading	Settle-ment (mm)	Cumul-ative settle-ment (mm)	Dial gauge reading	Settle-ment after rebound (mm)	Elastic rebound (mm)	Dial gauge reading	Settle-ment (mm)	Cumul-ative settle-ment (mm)	Dial gauge reading	Settle-ment after rebound (mm)	Elastic rebound (mm)	

TABLE 29.1

Cyclic Plate load test observations (Sheet No. 4)

Project Site location : Depth of Testing : Depth of water table : Date :

Load (kN)	Time	Settlement Dial gaugue-I						Settlement Dial Gauge - 1						Remarks
		During compression			During rebound at Zero load			During compression			During rebound at Zero load			
		Dial gauge reading	Settle-ment (mm)	Cumul-ative settle-ment (mm)	Dial gauge reading	Settle-ment after rebound (mm)	Elastic rebound (mm)	Dial gauge reading	Settle-ment (mm)	Cumul-ative settle-ment (mm)	Dial gauge reading	Settle-ment after rebound (mm)	Elastic rebound (mm)	

TABLE 29.1

Cyclic Plate load test observations (Sheet No. 5)

Project Site location : Depth of Testing : Depth of water table : Date :

Load (kN)	Time	Settlement Dial gaugue-I						Settlement Dial Gauge - 1						Remarks
		During compression			During rebound at Zero load			During compression			During rebound at Zero load			
		Dial gauge reading	Settle-ment (mm)	Cumul-ative settle-ment (mm)	Dial gauge reading	Settle-ment after rebound (mm)	Elastic rebound (mm)	Dial gauge reading	Settle-ment (mm)	Cumul-ative settle-ment (mm)	Dial gauge reading	Settle-ment after rebound (mm)	Elastic rebound (mm)	

30

BLOCK VIBRATION TEST TO DETERMINE COEFFICIENT OF ELASTIC UNIFORM COMPRESSION (C_u)

AIM

To determine the coefficient of elastic uniform compression (C_u) of soil at given site, by performing Block vibration test (Vertical vibration).

APPARATUS

1. **Mechanical Oscillator:** Mechanical Oscillator should be capable of producing a sinusoidally varying force and have a frequency range commensurate with the size of the block to be tested and type of the soil. It should have the provision for altering dynamic force level by simple adjustment of eccentric mass.
2. **DC Motor:** Motor of suitable power rating so as to run the above oscillator in the frequency range at full load. This should be of type that its own vibration are negligible.
3. **Speed control unit:** Speed control unit of capacity commensurate with dc motor, capable of operation at 220V ac input supply and giving variable dc voltage output. The maximum drop in voltage at full load should not exceed 2%.
4. **Displacement pick-up:** Three in number are required. Amplitudes may be directly measured using displacement pick-ups. These should be of appropriate capacity and should

have flat frequency response in the range 0 to 100 Hz or more and should be of high sensitivity; accuracy should be not less than 2%.

5. **Velocity pick-up:** Two in number, of suitable type, sensitive enough to record even feeble ground vibrations. Natural frequency 20 Hz and damping less than 1% of the critical damping.
6. **Universal amplifier:** Frequency response dc 100 Hz, high sensitivity with oscillograph which should not be less than 1V per chart line, maximum voltage gain should be 1500000; bridge exciter frequency should be 2000 Hz ± 5%.
7. **High gain dc amplifier:** To match velocity pick-up or geophone as the case may be.
8. **Phase meter:** Frequency range 5 to 100 Hz, phase difference 0 to 180° with a minimum accuracy of 1% at the centre and 3% at the ends. The input signal range may be 1mV to 5 V.
9. **Steel plate/Base for fixing oscillator and dc motor:** Thickness 20 mm, length and width depending upon size of oscillator unit.
10. Measuring tape
11. Apparatus for measuring field density of soil at site.

PROCEDURE

To perform block vibration test a concrete block with bolt embedded in it so as to mount the vibrating equipment on the block. The concrete block should be cast-in-situ at the site in a test pit having a depth equal to the depth of foundation. The dimensions of the concrete block, trial pit and other details are presented in the following paragraphs.

1. **Test pit:** A test of the size 4.5 × 2.75 m at the bottom and the depth equal to the proposed depth of foundations. All sides of the pit should be straight and vertical and bottom of the pit should be plane and horizontal.
2. **Test Block:** A plain cement concrete block of M15 concrete should be constructed in the test pit as shown in Fig. 30.1. The size of the block should be 1.5 × 0.75 × 0.70 m The concrete

block should be cured for at least 15 days before testing. Foundation bolts should be embedded into the concrete block at the time of casting for fixing the oscillator assembly. The location and dimensions of the bolts should be decided based on the base plate details of the oscillator assembly and the force expected to be exerted on the block. Special measures are taken to avoid any rigid coupling between the soil and the concrete block. Details of the test block are shown in Fig. 30.1

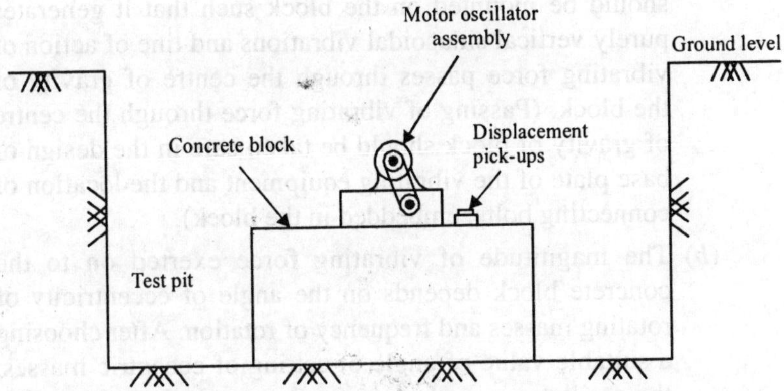

(*a*) Side view

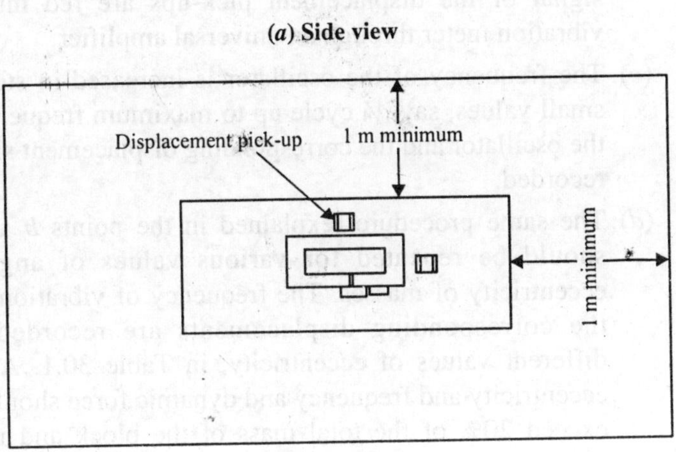

(b) Top view

Figure 30.1 : **Set-up for block vibration test (Vertical vibrations)**

3. **Test set up:** Mechanical oscillator and dc motor should be mounted on the concrete block with bolts and nuts so as to create vertical vibrations on to the block. Suitable connections between power supply, speed control unit, dc motor, amplifier and vibrating unit should be made as shown in Fig. 29.2.
4. **Test Procedure:**
   (*a*) Two displacement pick-ups should be fixed at the top of the block as shown in Fig. 29.1, such that they sense vertical motion of the block. The mechanical oscillator should be mounted on the block such that it generates purely vertical sinusoidal vibrations and line of action of vibrating force passes through the centre of gravity of the block. (Passing of vibrating force through the centre of gravity of block should be taken care in the design of base plate of the vibrating equipment and the location of connecting bolts, embedded in the block).

   (*b*) The magnitude of vibrating force exerted on to the concrete block depends on the angle of eccentricity of rotating masses and frequency of rotation. After choosing a suitable value of angle of setting of eccentric masses, the oscillator is made to run at a constant frequency. The signal of the displacement pick-ups are fed into the vibration meter through an universal amplifier.

   (*c*) The frequency of the oscillator is increased in steps of small values, say, ¼ cycle up to maximum frequency of the oscillator and the corresponding displacement signals recorded.

   (*d*) The same procedure (explained in the points *b* and *c*) should be repeated for various values of angle of eccentricity of masses. The frequency of vibrations and the corresponding displacements are recorded, for different values of eccentricity, in Table 30.1. At any eccentricity and frequency and dynamic force should not exceed 20% of the total mass of the block and motor oscillator assembly.The force exerted by the vibrator can be calculated based on the design of vibrating equipment.

For example one of the equations used for a vibrating equipment is as follows:

$$F = 4K\pi^2 f^2 \sin(\phi/2)$$

where

F = force of vibration (kg)

f = frequency of vibration (Hz)

ϕ = angle of eccentricity of moving masses

K = constant (0.0175); (the value of K depends on the equipment design).

TABLE 30.1

Observations of vertical block vibration Test to determine C_u for the site

Project Title :

Location of Site :

Soil Properties : Unit weight : ; Moisture content

Soil Type: Test pit Dimensions:

Block dimensions : ; Mass of Block + oscillator + motor :

Date of Casting of Block: ; Date of testing:

Position of pick-ups:

Test 1 : Angle of Eccentricity (°)

Frequency, f (Hz)	Displacement (mm)

Test 2 : Angle of Eccentricity (°) =

Frequency, f (Hz)	Displacement (mm)

Test 3 : Angle of Eccentricity (°)

Frequency, f (Hz)	Displacement (mm)

Test 4 : Angle of Eccentricity (°)

Frequency, f (Hz)	Displacement (mm)

Analysis of test result

1. Displacement amplitude versus frequency curve shall be plotted for each eccentricity of moving masses, to obtain the natural frequency of the soil and the foundation block tested. A typical plot is shown in Fig. 30.3. The natural frequency at different eccentricities will be different. (This is due to the fact that the effect of different eccentricities is to cause different strain levels below the block, which may be accounted for by choosing appropriate design parameters.)
2. Determination of coefficient of elastic uniform compression of soil: The coefficient of elastic uniform compression (C_u) of soil is given by the following equation:

$$C_u = 4\pi^2 f_{nz}^2 M/A \tag{30.1}$$

where

f_{nz} = Natural frequency under vertical vibrations

M = Mass of the block, oscillator and motor; and

A = Contact area of the block with the soil.

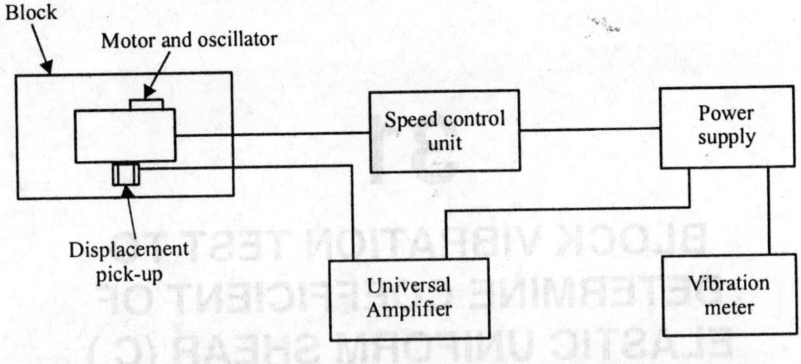

Figure 30.2 **: Block diagram of block vibration test (Vertical vibration)**

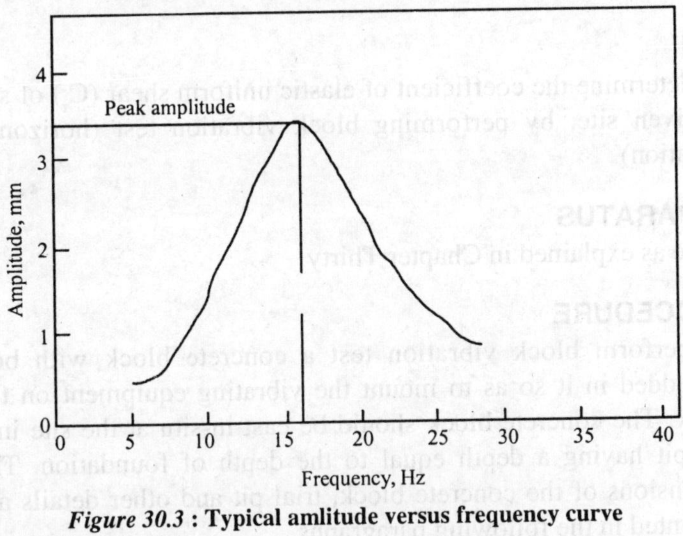

Figure 30.3 **: Typical amlitude versus frequency curve**

From the value of C_u obtained from Eq. (30.1) for the test block of contact area A the value of C_{u1} for the actual foundation having contact area of A_1 may be obtained from the equation:

$$C_{u1} = C_u \sqrt{(A/A_1)}$$

RESULT

Natural frequency of the soil-block system = Hz.

31

BLOCK VIBRATION TEST TO DETERMINE COEFFICIENT OF ELASTIC UNIFORM SHEAR (C_τ)

AIM

To determine the coefficient of elastic uniform shear (C_τ) of soil at given site, by performing block vibration test (horizontal vibration).

APPARATUS

Same as explained in Chapter Thirty.

PROCEDURE

To perform block vibration test a concrete block with bolt embedded in it so as to mount the vibrating equipment on the block. The concrete block should be cast-in-situ at the site in a test pit having a depth equal to the depth of foundation. The dimensions of the concrete block, trial pit and other details are presented in the following paragraphs.

5. **Test pit:** A test pit of the size 4.5 × 2.75 m at the bottom and the depth equal to the proposed depth of foundations. All sides of the pit should be straight and vertical and bottom of the pit should be plane and horizontal.
6. **Test Block:** A plain cement concrete block of M150 concrete should be constructed in the test pit as shown in Fig. 31.1. The size of the block should be 1.5 × 0.75 × 0.70 m. The concrete block should be cured for at least 15 days before

testing. Foundation bolts should be embedded into the concrete block at the time of casting for fixing the oscillator assembly. The location and dimensions of the bolts should be decided based on the base plate details of the oscillator assembly and the force expected to be exerted on the block. Special measures are taken to avoid any rigid coupling between the soil and the concrete block. Details of the test block are shown in Fig. 31.1.

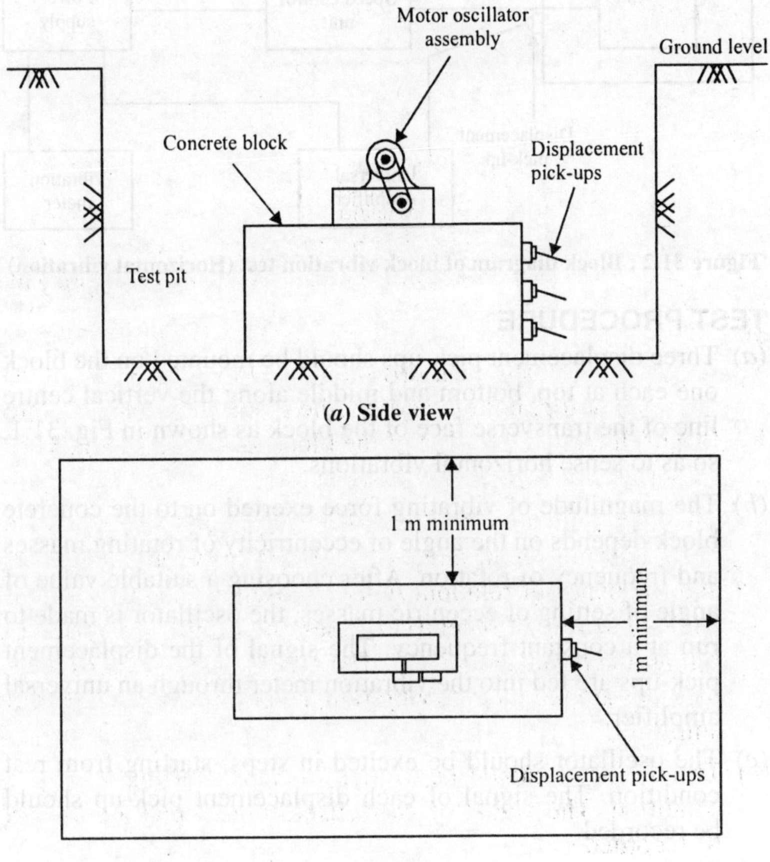

(b) Top view

Figure 31.1 **: Set-up for block vibration test (Horizontal vibrations)**

7. **Test set up:** Mechanical oscillator and dc motor should be mounted on the concrete block with bolts and nuts so that it generates horizontal sinusoidal vibrations in the direction of the longitudinal axis of the block. Suitable connections between power supply, speed control unit, dc motor, amplifier and vibrating unit should be made as shown in Fig. 31.2.

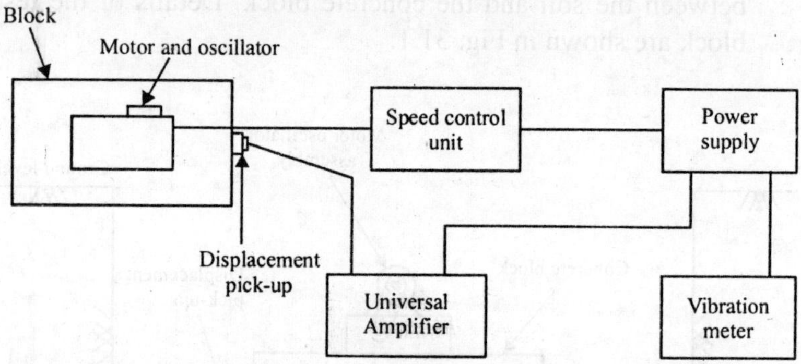

Figure 31.2 : Block diagram of block vibration test (Horizontal vibration)

TEST PROCEDURE

(*a*) Three displacement pick-ups should be mounted on the block one each at top, bottom and middle along the vertical centre line of the transverse face of the block as shown in Fig. 31.1, so as to sense horizontal vibrations.

(*b*) The magnitude of vibrating force exerted on to the concrete block depends on the angle of eccentricity of rotating masses and frequency of rotation. After choosing a suitable value of angle of setting of eccentric masses, the oscillator is made to run at a constant frequency. The signal of the displacement pick-ups are fed into the vibration meter through an universal amplifier.

(*c*) The oscillator should be excited in steps, starting from rest condition. The signal of each displacement pick-up should be recorded.

(*d*) The same procedure (explained in the points (*b*) and (*c*) should be repeated for various values of angle of eccentricity of masses. The frequency of vibrations and the corresponding displacements are recorded, for different values of eccentricity, in Table 31.1

OBSERVATIONS

TABLE 31.1

Observations of horizontal block vibration test to determine C_t for the site

Project Title : Location of Site :

Soil Properties : Unit weight : ; Moisture content :

Soil Type : Test pit Dimensions : ;

Block dimensions : ; Mass of Block + oscillator + motor :

Date of Casting of Block : ; Date of testing :

Position of pick-ups (distance from the base of the Block) :

Distance of Displacement pick-up No. 1 (at top) =

Distance of Displacement pick-up No. 2 (at middle) =

Distance of Displacement pick-up No. 3 (at bottom) =

Test 1 : Angle of Eccentricity (°) =

Frequency, f (Hz)	Displacement (mm)		
	At Top Pick-up. No. 1	At Middle Pick-up. No. 2	At Bottom Pick-up. No. 3

Test 2 : Angle of Eccentricity (°) =

Frequency, f (Hz)	Displacement (mm)		
	At Top Pick-up. No. 1	At Middle Pick-up. No. 2	At Bottom Pick-up. No. 3

Test 3 : Angle of Eccentricity (°) =

Frequency, f (Hz)	Displacement (mm)		
	At Top Pick-up. No. 1	At Middle Pick-up. No. 2	At Bottom Pick-up. No. 3

Test 4 : Angle of Eccentricity (°) =

Frequency, f (Hz)	Displacement (mm)		
	At Top Pick-up. No. 1	At Middle Pick-up. No. 2	At Bottom Pick-up. No. 3

CALCULATIONS

Determination of mode of vibration: Amplitude versus height of the block shall be plotted at natural frequency of the system from the analysis of data from the pick-up mounted at different locations along the vertical face of the block. Typical plots are shown in Fig. 31.3. If the plot obtained corresponds to Fig. 31.3(*a*), then the natural frequency corresponds to first mode or lower natural frequency. On the other hand, if it corresponds to that in Fig. 31.3 (*b*), then the natural frequency corresponds to second mode or higher natural frequency.

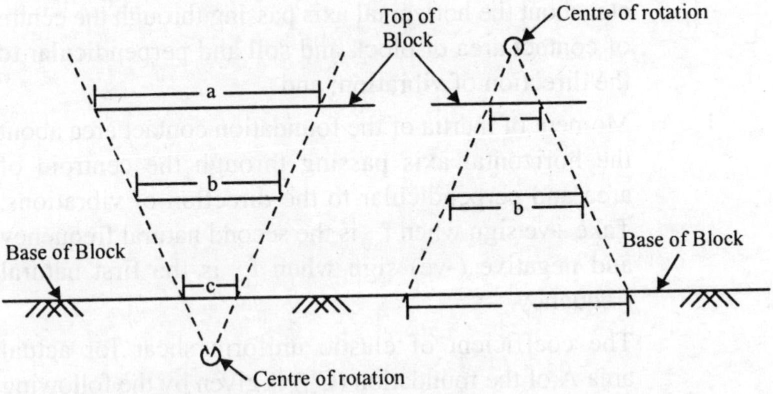

(*a*) First mode of vibration **(*b*) Second mode of vibration**

a - Double amplitude of top pick-up;

b - Double amplitude of middle pick-up;

c - Double amplitude of bottom pick-up.

Figure 31.3 **: Determination of mode of vibration**

Determination of coefficient of elastic uniform shear of soil: The coefficient of elastic uniform shear (C_τ) of soil is given by the following equation;

$$(C_\tau) = 8\pi 2_\gamma f^2_{nx} / [(A_o + I_o) \pm \sqrt{((A_o + I_o)^2 - 4\gamma A_o I_o)}] \quad (31.1)$$

where

γ = $M_m/M_{m\theta}$

f_{nx} = Horizontal resonant frequency of block soil system;

A_o = A/M

A = Contact area of block with soil

M = Mass of concrete block, oscillator and motors

I_o = $3.46\, I/M_{m\theta}$

M_m = Mass moment inertial of block, oscillator, motor, etc., about the horizontal axis passing through the centre of gravity of block and perpendicular to the direction of vibration;

$M_{m\theta}$ = Mass moment of inertia of the block, oscillator, motor, etc. about the horizontal axis passing through the centre of contact area of block and soil and perpendicular to the direction of vibration; and

I = Moment of inertia of the foundation contact area about the horizontal axis passing through the centroid of area and perpendicular to the direction of vibrations.

Take +ve sign when f_{nx} is the second natural frequency and negative (-ve) sign when f_{nx} is the first natural frequency.

The coefficient of elastic uniform shear for actual area A_l of the foundation ($C_{\tau l}$) is given by the following equation

$$C_{\tau l} = C_\tau \sqrt{\{A/A_l\}}$$

RESULTS:

Resonance frequency:

Mode of Vibration:

Coefficient of elastic uniform shear:

32

BLOCK VIBRATION TEST TO DETERMINE DAMPING COEFFICIENT OF SOIL (ξ)

AIM

To determine the damping coefficient (ξ) of soil at given site, by performing Block vibration test (vertical vibration).

APPARATUS

Same as explained in Chapter 30.

PROCEDURE

Apparatus set up and the test procedure is same as explained in Chapter Twenty nine.

OBSERVATIONS AND CALCULATIONS:

After obtaining the frequency versus amplitude curve, compute the Damping coefficient (ξ) of soil using the following equation.

$$\xi = (f_2 - f_1)/(2f_{nz})$$

where

f_1, f_2 = two frequencies at which the amplitude is equal to $X_m/(\sqrt{2})$

X_m = maximum amplitude

f_{nz} = frequency at which the amplitude is maximum (see Fig. 31.1)

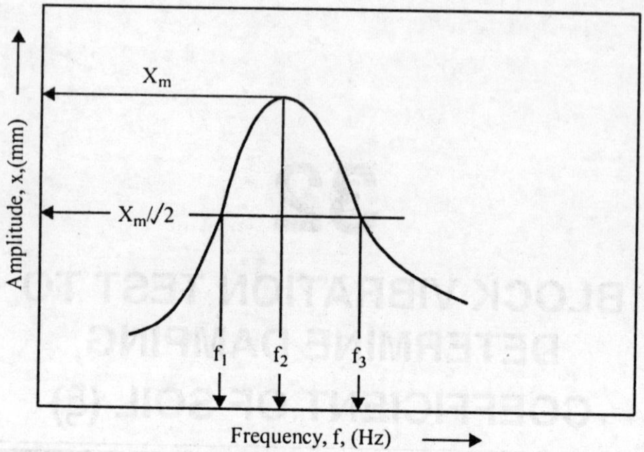

Figure 32.1 **: Determination of damping coefficient of soil**

RESULT

Damping coefficient of Soil =

33

BLOCK VIBRATION TEST TO DETERMINE THE ELASTIC MODULUS (E) AND SHEAR MODULUS (G_S)

AIM

To determine Elastic modulus (E) and Shear modulus (G_s) of soil.

THEORY

In case of uniform soil extending upto infinite depth, the wave length of propagating vibrations is given by:

$$\lambda/4 = S$$

where

λ = wavelength in cm,

S = measured distance between the two geophones when the phase difference between them is 90°.

Velocity of shear wave V_s is given by:

$$V_s = \lambda f$$

where

f = frequency of vibration at which the wavelength has been measured.

Shear wave velocity through the soil media is used to estimate the elastic and shear modulus of soil.

APPARATUS

Same as explained in Chapter Twenty six.

PROCEDURE

To perform block vibration test a concrete block with bolt embedded in it so as to mount the vibrating equipment on the block. The concrete block should be cast-in-situ at the site in a test pit having a depth equal to the depth of foundation. The dimensions of the concrete block, trial pit and other details are presented in Chapter Thirty.

1. **Test set Up:** Mechanical oscillator and dc motor should be mounted on the concrete block with bolts and nuts so as to create vertical vibrations on the block. Suitable connections between power supply, speed control unit, dc motor, amplifier and vibrating unit should be made as shown in Fig. 30.1.

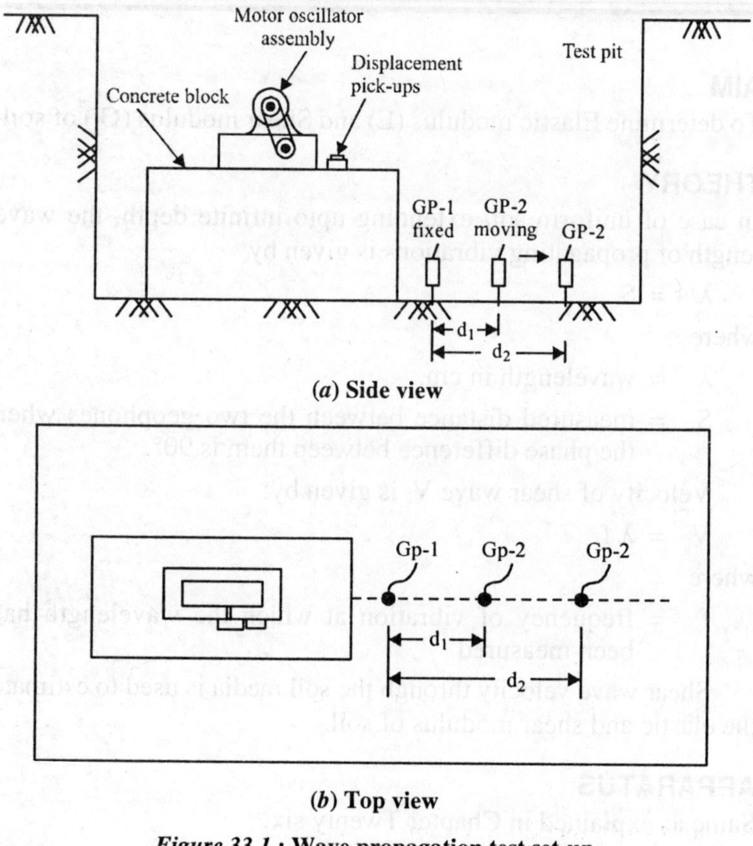

Figure 33.1 **: Wave propagation test set-up**

2. **Test Procedure:**

   (*a*) Two Geophones, say GP-1 and GP-2, are connected to the phase meter (build-in with the vibration meter) through universal amplifier. The mechanical oscillator should be mounted on the block such that it generates purely vertical sinusoidal vibrations and line of action of vibrating force passes through the centre of gravity of the block.

   (*b*) Draw a line on the ground along the longitudinal axis of the block. Fix the first geophone GP-1 near the block to sense the vertical vibrations of the ground. On the line drawn, mark the positions for the second geophone, at an interval of approximately 0.3 m (say 0.3 m, 0.6 m, 0.9 m etc.) from first geophone GP-1. Fix the second geophone in its position (i.e. 0.3 m away from the first geophone) as shown in Fig. 33.1

   (*c*) After choosing a suitable value of angle of setting of eccentric masses, the oscillator is made to run at a constant frequency. Under steady state vibration condition record the phase difference between the vibrations at the two geophones (PD_1) and the corresponding distance between the two geophones (d_1).

   (*d*) Keeping the GP-1 in its position, move the GP-2 to its next position (i.e. about 0.6 m) away from GP-1. Record the phase difference PD_2 and the corresponding distance between the two geophones (d_2).

   (*e*) The procedure is repeated for various values of d and the corresponding PD recorded till the PD exceeds 90° or $\pi/2$ radians.

Record the observations in Table 33.1. Repeat the experiment at different frequencies of vibrations and angle of eccentricities.

Precautions: It may be noted that, the object taking different set of readings is to obtain the distance between the geophones, d, which provides a phase difference of $\pi/2$ radians. Hence, the distance between the geophones should be increased from a minimum value depending on the type of soil. The values suggested above are only for guidelines.

OBSERVATIONS

TABLE 33.1

Observations for wave propagation test

Project Title : Location of Site :

Soil Properties : Unit weight : ; Moisture content : Soil Type:

Position of first geophone from the face of the block:

Trial 1 (Frequency of Testing : Hz)

Distance between Geophones, d (cm)	Phase difference, PD (°)

Trial 2 (Frequency of Testing : Hz)

Distance between Geophones, d (cm)	Phase difference, PD (°)

Trial 3 (Frequency of Testing : Hz)

Distance between Geophones, d (cm)	Phase difference, PD (°)

CALCULATIONS

From the observations made in Table 33.1 draw a graph for the distance between the geophones and the corresponding phase difference of the wave as shown in Fig. 33.2. Obtain the distance S corresponding to a phase difference of 90°. The distance $S = \lambda/4$.

Calculate the wavelength $\lambda = 4S$.

Knowing the wave length λ and the corresponding frequency of vibration, f the velocity of shear wave V_s is given by

$$V_s = \lambda f.$$

where

f = frequency of vibration at which the wave length has been calculated.

The elastic modulus E and shear modulus G of the soil medium is calculated as follows:

$$E = 2\gamma V_s^2 (1 + \varepsilon)$$

$$G = \gamma V_s^2$$

where

γ = unit weight of soil,

V_s = velocity of shear waves, and

ε = Poisson's ratio of soil.

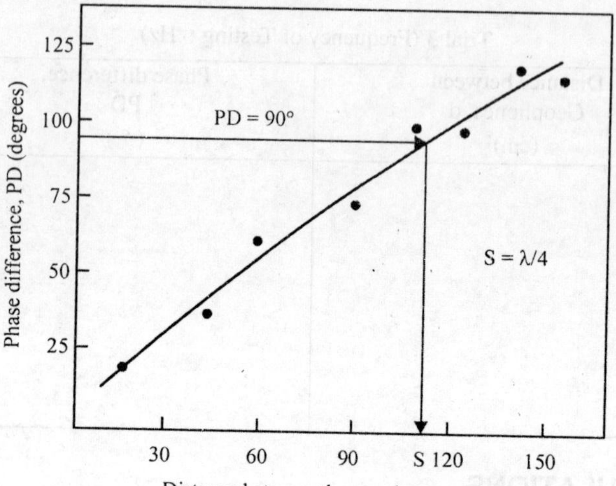

***Figure 33.2* : Graph showing distance between geophones Vs phase difference**

TABLE 33.2

Poisson's ratios of different soils

Type of soil	Poisson's ratio, ε
Clay	0.5
Sand	0.30 to 0.35
Rock	0.15 to 0.25